SNOWSPORT SCOTLAND

ALPINE SKI LEADER
OFFICIAL TRAINING MANUAL

Drew Michie

Derek Tate

Design and production:
White Spider Ltd.
2 Tay Street,
Edinburgh, EH11 1EA
info@whitespiderltd.co.uk
www.whitespiderltd.co.uk

Published and distributed in the UK by:
Snowsport Scotland
Caledonia House, South Gyle
Edinburgh, EH12 9DQ
info@snowsportscotland.org
www.snowsportscotland.org

ISBN: 978-0-9567478-0-8
Snowsport Scotland Alpine Ski Leader Official Training Manual

Front cover skiers in action; Shona Tate, Snowsport Scotland Tutor and Toby Fishel, www.developyourskiing.com
The other two pictures are of ASL courses taking place in Grimentz (Switzerland) and Pila (Italy).

contents

authors

Drew Michie

Drew Michie has been a professional footballer, PE Teacher and an Adviser in Outdoor Education for a Scottish Local Education Authority. During this professional career he developed an interest in Coach Education and started to train and assess Kayak instructors in the early 1970's He was also Chairman of the Scottish Canoe Association Coaching Committee during that decade.

In the 1980's Drew's interest in Alpine Skiing saw him become Chairman of Snowsport Scotland Coaching Committee. Around that time Drew gained an Alpine Ski Leader award plus a range of BASI awards. Since the 1990's Drew has been delivering Alpine Ski Leader Courses for Snowsport Scotland.

In the early 1990's Drew, along with three colleagues wrote the Scottish Mountain Bike Leader scheme for Scottish Cycling which has grown immensely, has become the market leader and now operates throughout the UK and abroad. Until recently Drew was Chair of the Scottish Mountain Bike Leader Association.

Drew has been an active hill walker and has qualifications in hill walking and rock climbing to compliment other Outdoor Education qualifications.

Drew has been a member of the Scottish Advisory Panel for Outdoor Education since 1986 and has also been involved as a committee member with the UK Adventure Activity Industry Advisory Committee, The Scottish Mountain Safety Forum and the Scottish Adventure Activity Forum. In 2003 he was co-author of the Scottish Government's publication "Health and Safety on Educational Excursions". Drew has also written a book on "Orienteering in the 5-14 Curriculum" and has just completed a book on "Bike Games" for Trail Cycle Leaders.

Drew has brought a wealth of broad outdoor education experience to the preparation of this Coaching Scheme Manual

Derek Tate

Derek Tate has been teaching skiing full time since 1987. Since then he has worked in various locations around the world including; Scotland, France, Switzerland, Austria, Germany and the USA.

During the 1990's Derek worked extensively for the Scottish National Ski Council (now Snowsport Scotland) bringing coaching scheme qualifications in line with SNVQs. He was also Manager at Firpark Ski Centre in Tillicoultry where he developed the class structure and the race training programme.
Derek qualified through the BASI system to Level 4 ISTD and is a current trainer for the British Association of Snowsport Instructors where he trains and assesses instructors' right through to Level 4 modules.

Derek has also been instrumental in developing the qualification system for the "Irish Association of Snowsports Instructors (IASI)". He is the current Head of Training for the Association and will be leading the Irish delegation to the Interski Congress in St. Anton, Austria in January 2011.

In 2007 Parallel Dreams Alpine Skiing was published and Derek was principal author and editor of this book. This publication was endorsed by IASI and is used as their technical reference manual.

Together with his wife Shona (also a BASI & IASI Trainer) Derek now runs his own ski school, BASS Chamonix & Megeve, and is based in Les Bossons just outside Chamonix town. Much of his work these days is delivering off piste and backcountry skiing courses which has become a real passion.

Derek has brought a wealth of technical experience to help contribute to the preparation of this Coaching Scheme Manual.

foreward

Snowsport Scotland:
Coaching Handbook, 2010

Foreword

I felt very honoured when asked by Kenny King of Snowsport Scotland if I would write this introduction to the new Training Manual for the Alpine Ski Leader Scheme; later reflecting that the request could have been made because it was thought I had 'been in it since the beginning'. However, as the first recorded instance of skiing in Scotland is said to have been in 1892, I have to say this is something of an exaggeration.

Nevertheless, I do remember very clearly my first day on Cairngorm in January 1964, in company with a group of Glasgow schoolboys from Glenmore Lodge and under the instruction of Norman 'Plum' Worral. Among the gems he shared with me, no doubt to give a fillip to my flagging morale as I crept nervously down Car Park Gully without any of the dashing flair of my younger fellow novices, was that he had taken much longer learning how to ski slowly under control than to learn to ski fast. I also recall later the same week descending the upper slopes of Corrie Cas, by then being instructed by another founding legend of Scottish ski teaching, Jack Thomson, recognising with great pleasure that I could actually turn my ploughing skis in both directions, possibly a life changing moment?

Whether it was or not, I have recognised since that all of us skiing down the Corrie that day were part of the great post World War 2 expansion of interest in Britain in many outdoor activities, including skiing, all of these having experienced unprecedented growth in numbers of participants during the previous two decades. In addition, whereas in earlier eras well established clubs for these pursuits, national and local, had coped quite effectively with the comparative trickle of new recruits, from the 1950s onward much greater numbers necessitated the establishment of new avenues for instruction and reorganisation of national bodies, often with the aid of some state funding.

In the case of skiing in the Highlands, with the benefits of a long series of snowy winters and the building of the first professionally engineered lifts, courses of training were established for seasonal full-timers by the British Association of Professional Ski Instructors (BAPSI, later BASI). Also, the British Ski Instruction Council launched the Ski Leader scheme for the many teachers, youth leaders and others involved in leading young people onto snow on an occasional, and usually voluntary, basis. For the first Ski Leader weeks, held at Glenmore Lodge in 1966 and 1967, BASI provided the trainers on snow, the six-day courses involving five days of ski training, with evening lecture and workshop sessions and one day of assessment. As one of those early candidates on a course in May, 1967, our group enjoyed what I remember being a wonderful week, instructed by Clive Freshwater on beautiful snow; my snow ploughing having really come on well during the previous 3 years.

Some years later, in the 1980s, the Scottish National Ski Council (SNSC) moved from its dependence on BASI Trainers for staffing ski leader courses, developing a cadre of its own tutors and impelling future candidates into taking more responsibility for their own and others' learning by leading the delivery of some of the course material. In addition, aspiring leaders would be assessed for technical skiing competence prior to the course, on which assessment would be continuous. This meant that on a course the tutor and candidates could spend much more time examining the key areas of competence associated with teaching and leading on and off the snow, a successful general pattern which has continued until the present time.

A further development for those conducting courses within the SNSC scheme, spurred on by the deterioration in snow cover on Scottish mountains during most winters since the 1980s, allied to the emergence of low cost airlines, has been the expansion in the numbers of courses run in the Alps, and even in North America. Although at first this was viewed sceptically by some, there have been many benefits with comparatively few problems. Also, it has had to be recognised that most of the newly emerging leaders wherever they come from in the UK or elsewhere, have been impelled increasingly to operate abroad with their groups.

However, after all this, the major development affecting every outdoor activity over the last 20 years has been the increasing requirement by government and society at large for leaders of groups out of doors to show clearly that every conceivable risk has been assessed effectively prior to and during each venture. As with other changes the SNSC, aided and supported particularly in this instance by the Scottish local authorities through their outdoor advisory panel (SAPOE), has been extremely effective in incorporating and modifying course structures and content as required by these new demands, ensuring that without sacrificing the enjoyment of participants, leaders continue to demonstrate sound and safe practice to the highest standards.

As a technical basis for those earliest ski leader courses, and also for candidates on BASI courses at the same time, the then recently published and comprehensive Official American Ski Technique was employed as a reference. Although this was a well-written and clearly illustrated manual, it was naturally not aimed at conditions in Britain and was superseded in 1973 by the first BASI Manual, supplemented for some aspects by the Mountain Leadership Handbook ('Langmuir'). However, neither of these works included a focus on the special problems facing leaders of groups of schoolchildren and other learners on skis, so increasingly a range of specific handouts were developed along with the courses, revised and photocopied many times over the years and later being loosely bound into booklets.

foreward

With all this attention to overall developments in snow sports, and what might be described as 'the mechanics' of The Scheme, it is easy to forget the most important role which ski leaders have filled so effectively over the years; introducing novices safely and enjoyably to experiences on snow and providing that spark that imbues them with a life-long enthusiasm for the sport of their choice. It is to the enormous credit of the team which has written and produced this excellent new Coaching Manual that, while it has drawn widely on the past, it has also worked to great effect in providing the most up to date advice and guidance into which have been incorporated fresh inspiration for both current and future leaders.

Finally, with stiff competition from other agencies and schemes for the custom of those who wish to learn how to lead others in the early stages of their careers on skis, why is it that SNSC courses remain so appealing to the many who attend each year, sometimes through 'refreshers', even maintaining their involvement over several decades? After reading through some of the recent feedback provided after each course, without a doubt in my mind it is the quality of both the courses and the tutors which continue to provide the bulk of this appeal. Many graduates testify to both the stimulation and challenges provided by the courses and the skills and professionalism of the staff, as well as improvements in both their technique on snow and the increased expertise they develop in the guidance of others. With all this, allied to the robust foundations provided by this new manual, there seems little doubt that the vital enthusiasm referred to above will continue to be sparked in many future generations of skiers.

John Cheesmond
September 2010

John Cheesmond, formerly Senior Lecturer in Outdoor Education at both Dunfermline College and Moray House College of Education, entered the professional outdoor life in 1963 from a background in mountaineering. He was soon drawn into alpine skiing which he has pursued with great enthusiasm since, through a long career in teaching whilst at the same time working through the BASI system.

As part of his professional involvement in the sport he was one of a small group of SNSC Coaching Committee members, including the late John Hynes, who redesigned the Ski Leader scheme in 1987. John continued his involvement not only at the development stages but also as a well respected Tutor of Alpine Ski Leader courses into the 1990's.

acknowledgements

Snowsport Scotland would like to acknowledge the help given in preparation and production of this course Manual.

The principal authors were Derek Tate (Technical Chapter) and Drew Michie (all other Chapters) The following helped by providing feedback and guidance on draft chapters and their input in this regard is greatly appreciated. They are

Ian Linklater (Technical and Teaching)
Kenny King (First Aid and Hypothermia)
Mark Diggins Scottish Avalanche Information Service (Mountain Safety)
Scottish Cycling (some of the material in this book is based on work originally produced by Drew Michie for Scottish Cycling for publication in the SMBLA (now called MBLA) Manual
Gavin Howat Health and Safety Executive (Health and Safety)
Ken Ogilvie (Author "Leading and Managing Groups in the Outdoors") for allowing some of the models and styles of leadership to be based on his original work.
Eric Davies Salomon GB for use of the Salomon Release Value Chart on page 159

Photographs: Derek Tate (Parallel Dreams) and Drew Michie
                Duggi Bryce (Page 32)
                Mark Diggins (Page 133)

introduction

By the end of this section all candidates should be able to:

- State the origins of the scheme
- Describe the awards and what you need to do to take part
- Outline a course
- State the competencies required for assessment

1 ORIGINS OF THE SCHEME

The first awards were introduced in Season 1966 - 67 and courses were originally organised by the British Ski Instruction Council (BSIC) which was formed in 1966 as an arbitration body of the interested parties concerned with ski instruction in Britain. These were: The National Ski Federation of Great Britain, The Scottish National Ski Council (SNSC), The British Association of Professional Ski Instructors (BAPSI), The Association of Ski Schools in Great Britain, The Central Council of Physical Recreation, and the Scottish Council of Physical Recreation. In 1966 the Council (BSIC) was involved in the process of agreeing standards for Ski Schools and of formulating grades of Ski Instructor

The grades agreed for Scotland were:
Grade 1. Full member BAPSI
Grade 2. Associate Member of BAPSI
Grade 3. Assistant Instructor BAPSI - Senior Ski Leader
Grade 4. Ski Leader

Six courses were arranged in Scotland for all grades with preparatory two day selection courses taking place at Hillend under the direction of Hans Kuwall, for a fee of 10/- (50p in new money). There were twenty places per course.The courses were organised jointly by SNSC and SCPR with BAPSI providing the trainers. The course literature stated:

"It should be understood that every participant is expected to be able to ski precisely and neatly, and preferably up to parallel standard, though only authorised to teach up to stem Christie standard in the lower qualifications"

"At Glenmore Lodge, Aviemore, Grade IV - Ski Leaders. These one week courses are designed to help school teachers and youth leaders who intend to introduce boys and girls to skiing. Before acceptance for the course candidates must be able to demonstrate linked stem turns and side slipping. On completion of a course a successful candidate will be awarded a certificate of competence."

"Dates: December 17th to 23rd 1966
April 22nd to 29th 1967
April 29th to May 6th 1967
Fee: for one week courses with accommodation and without lifts £11. 11s."

Candidates could expect to be planning their courses from a course brochure like the one below.

SKI INSTRUCTOR'S COURSES 1966-67

British Ski Instruction Council

CERTIFICATE of INSTRUCTION

This is to certify that

Margaret Taylor Scobbie

has attended a B.S.I.C. Instructors' Course

from *22nd April 1967* to *28th April 1967*

and has qualified as a *Ski Leader*

Signed _____

EXAMINER

BRITISH SKI INSTRUCTION COUNCIL

The above details were supplied by Margaret and Niall Scobbie and John Cheesmond who were all early recipients of the award.

In 1987 the scheme changed and the award was rebranded the Alpine Ski Leader Award. The courses changed to become 7 days continuous training and assessment with one course tutor throughout. This change was negotiated with BASI, who still supplied the trainers, and an agreement was signed.

Eventually Snowsport Scotland developed its own Course Tutors and by the mid 1990's courses were being delivered entirely by Snowsport Scotland Tutors, some of whom were also BASI Trainers. Courses now take place throughout Europe and in North America.

2 TUTORS

All Tutors are registered with Snowsport Scotland and provide courses on behalf of Snowsport Scotland. Tutors may be employed by a local authority or by a commercial ski travel company, or they may work independently, but they all operate to the same guidelines, course structure and syllabus agreed by the awarding body.

During their qualification, Snowsport Scotland Tutors undertake Coach Educator Tutor Training Course provided by Sportscotland approved Trainers, and become competent to Tutor status through an apprenticeship lasting approximately 12-18 months during which they are supported by a Mentor Tutor. Some Tutors hold equivalent qualifications in other outdoor activities such as canoeing, mountaineering, mountain biking and climbing.

A full list of Tutors is available from the Snowsport Scotland by contacting the Snowsport Scotland office.

3 AWARDS

3.1 Alpine Ski Leader (ASL)

The Scottish Alpine Ski Leader qualification is widely recognised throughout the UK as the most appropriate award for skiers taking sole charge of groups (often children) in the mountain environment. The Alpine Ski Leader is an award originally developed in the 1960's, mainly for teachers and youth workers wishing to introduce skiing to young people from their own organisation, often without direct financial remuneration. The award covers a range of responsibilities including; planning, organising, supervising, leading and teaching.

The key elements of an Alpine Ski Leader course are:
- Leadership
- Technical skiing
- Teaching
- Mountain skills

3.2 Scope of the Award

This award offers the opportunity to gain technical competence in leading and teaching within the bounds of a resort in a mountain environment at home and abroad. It does not provide a professional instruction qualification and does not permit a Leader to take their group off piste.

It is the combination of personal leadership qualities, leadership skills, technical and teaching skills which form the basis of effective group management in a skiing environment and the award assesses all these elements.

As part of leading their group it may be necessary for a Leader to teach the group skills. A Leader is licensed and insured to teach their own group. A leader may operate anywhere within the remit of the award. The award is limited to those travelling and working with their own groups and would be invalid if used in any other circumstances.

When operating abroad, a Leader should introduce themselves to the local snowsports school and inform them of their intentions whilst leading in a resort. This is good practice and strongly recommended by Snowsport Scotland

The course contains elements designed to improve the participant's ability to lead skiers in a mountain environment and to introduce skiing to children in a safe and enjoyable manner.

4 ENTRY REQUIREMENTS

Course participants should:
- Be at least 18 years of age
- Be able to make parallel turns on groomed red runs in good conditions showing effective balance and control.
- Have at least 20 days on-snow experience
- Use carving skis
- Understand all levels of the UK Snowsport Awards and be able to perform many of the activites.
- Be a member of the Snowsport Scotland Coaching Scheme.

Anyone unsure of their level of performance should seek the advice of a qualified instructor prior to enrolling for a course.

5 FIRST AID QUALIFICATION

For any Snowsport Scotland award to become and remain valid, Leaders must hold an appropriate first aid qualification. Candidates not presenting evidence of valid first aid training at the time of registration will be automatically "deferred"; and must submit a copy of their first aid qualification to Snowsport Scotland before an Alpine Ski Leadership certificate can be awarded.

Accepted first aid training courses should be provided by organisations approved by HSE for the purpose of first aid training, and delivered by staff who are registered with that organisation as first aid trainers or assessors. Courses must be a minimum of 12 hours, with no sessions shorter than 2 hours, and should contain material relevant to the outdoor environment.

First Aid Courses must include:
- action at an incident
- management of an unconscious casualty
- resuscitation
- treatment and control of bleeding
- treatment of injuries to bones, muscles and joints.
- recognition and treatment of shock
- treatment of choking
- recognition and treatment of common illnesses
- contents of first aid kits

A list of approved first aid providers can be found in the Useful Contacts section of the Snowsport Scotland website.

introduction

6 SNOWSPORT SCOTLAND MEMBERSHIP

Those attending courses require to join the Snowsport Scotland Coaching Scheme. Membership is required for entry to any Snowsport Scotland course.

Please note that membership of the Snowsport Scotland scheme needs to be renewed annually in September. Failure to renew means that your qualification is not valid and you will not be covered by the Snowsport Scotland Insurance or included on the list of qualified members.

The benefits for members of the Coaching Scheme are:
- Civil liability insurance (third party & professional indemnity).
- Inclusion on the list of qualified leaders, instructors and coaches as circulated to schools, clubs, local authorities etc.
- Special equipment and clothing offers when available.
- Access to reciprocal rights in Alpine huts and benefits from the BMC.
- Representation at National and British levels.
- Invitation to the Snowsport Scotland Coaches Forum.
- Access to Snowsport Scotland reference library (articles, magazines, books, videos, etc.).
- Snowsport Scotland Annual Report (on request).
- Country wide access to UK Snowsports courses

To register with the Coaching Scheme visit the Snowsport Scotland web site and print out the membership form, complete it and sign it and post together with the registration fee, direct debit form, a photocopy of your first aid certificate, and a passport photo to Snowsport Scotland, Caledonia House, South Gyle Edinburgh EH12 9DQ. (can be emailed if you have a digital copy to info@snowsportscotland.org)

7 COURSES

7.1 Course Content

The content of the course includes:

Leadership skills
Group leading considerations; group practice supervision; knowledge of ski resorts.

Mountain skills
Navigation; weather; accident procedures.

Technical skills
Personal performance;

Teaching Skills
Knowledge of instructional methods; introducing skiing to children;

Presentation Skills
The ability to gather and present information

The course material is presented primarily during on-snow skiing sessions and is supported by evening programmes and seminar sessions. The course provides opportunities for discussion and candidates are required to deliver a short presentation (a topic is sent to participants at least 14 days prior to the start of the course).

Courses normally last for 7 days however if a course takes place in the Alps where there is the likelihood of getting onto the hill every day it can be run over 6 days. Assessment of the course is continual during the six/seven days of the course. The course Tutor will provide ongoing feedback during the course concerning participant's performance. On completion of the course the Tutor will conduct individual course reviews with each participant.

The outcomes of the course can be "Pass, Fail or a Deferral (if only one element has been unsuccessful). A deferral will mean a reassessment of that element in line with Snowsport Scotland's Resit Policy.

There is a maximum of 10 candidates per course.

7.2 Model Training Courses & Learning Outcomes

To ensure consistency in the delivery of training Snowsport Scotland has designed a draft Model course programme. This course is built around small learning sessions, each one with clear learning outcomes.Tutors may run a slightly modified course due to weather conditions and resort differences but they should still be delivering the standard learning outcomes.

7.2.1 Draft Model Programme (6 day version)

Morning On snow	Afternoon On snow	Afternoon Off snow	Evening Off snow	
			Session i - Course Induction	
Session 2 - Find Ski Legs - Fundamentals - Posture and Steering	Session 3 - Video of Performance - Straight Running	Daily Review Presentations 1,2, 3 & 4	Session 4 - Video Feedback Session 5 (part 1) - Progression Video	DAY 1

Session 6
- Introductory Session
	Session 5 (part 2)
	- Progression from
	  from Beginner
	  to Parallel
		Daily Review
		
		Presentations
		5, 6 & 7
			Session 7
			- Action Centred
			  Leadership
				DAY 2

Session 8 - Leading Activity (1)	Session 9 - Fault Finding - Making Pictures Match Words	Daily Review Presentations 8, 9 & 10	Individual Feedback Session10 (part 1) - Lesson Planning	DAY 3
Session 11 - Personal Performance	Session10 (part 2) - Lesson Delivery & evaluation	Session 10 (part 3) - Video review of lesson Session 12 - Roles & Qualities of ASL	Session 13 - Mosston's Teaching Styles Session 14 - Snow & Avalanche	DAY 4
Session 15 - Leading Activity (2)	Clinics	Daily Review Worksheet Session Course Evaluation	Lesson Planning for assessment	DAY 5
Preparation on snow for Teaching Assessment	Teaching Assessment	Course Results and Candidate Debrief Course Review		DAY 6

7.2.2 Additional Modules

Some Tutors can provide additional voluntary
modules/additions to the course. These are:
- Salomon Rental Binding Adjustment
  (Certified by Salomon GB)
- Ski Maintenance
- Ski Patrol visit

If these modules can be made available your Tutor
will inform you at the start of the course and time to
include them negotiated.

7.2.3 Learning Outcomes for programme on previous page

Alpine Ski Leader Course Learning Outcomes
By the end of each session you will be able to:

Session 1
- Describe the structure of your course
- State our domestic arrangements & daily programme
- Explain the presentation timetable
- Recognise the "fundamentals" of skiing

Session 2
- Describe how to find your ski-ing legs
- State two of the fundamentals used
- List exercises to help improve posture
  and balance

Session 3
- Explain how to improve posture when
  "straight running"

Session 4
- Describe what you look like when
  "straight running"

Session 5
- State the stages in the "Progression from
  Beginner to Parallel"
- Explain key points in demonstrating them

Session 6
- State the stages you might expect to take a
  beginner through

- List a range of activities for beginner sessions
- Describe how to Make it "fun"

Session 7
- Name one Leadership model
- State when a particular change in leadership style would be appropriate

Sessions 8 & 15
- Lead a small group on the hill
- List some key pointers for good leadership
- Outline some key steps to ensure your group are kept together
- Identify when to vary your leadership style

Session 9
- Describe common skiing faults
- State corrective practices
- Describe how effectively you demonstrate

Session 10
- Plan a lesson
- Conduct a lesson
- Evaluate a lesson

Session 11
- Describe the what the difference between skiddy and grippy turns feels like
- State what to do to ski fast in control

Session 12
- List the skills, knowledge and qualities of an Alpine Ski Leader

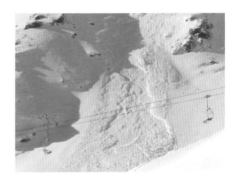

Session 13
- List adult learning principles
- Identify a range of teaching styles and state how they might be used, including:-
  Command, Practice, Reciprocal, Self-check, Inclusion and Convergent (guided discovery)

Session 14
- Describe how a snow pack is formed
- Describe how the layers can slide on one another
- State how to assess a slope for safety
- Explain how an avalanche is triggered
- List how to behave if you are caught in an avalanche
- List how to react if you see someone caught in an avalanche

introduction

7.3 COMPETENCIES

An attempt has been made to create a tool for identifying various competencies. The tables following are set out in a style, where each key area is expanded into key elements. Each element has performance components which should help in understanding what is meant by each element. This table is included to assist in understanding the competencies required by an Alpine Ski Leader.

7.3.1 Leadership

LEADERSHIP ELEMENTS	PERFORMANCE COMPONENTS
1. Managing a Group Safely and Effectively	1. Obtains sound relationship 2. Takes sensible decisions on safety 3. Keeps control 4. Keeps everyone informed 5. Keeps in touch with whole group
2. Making Decisions	1. Considers all relevant factors 2. Doesn't avoid difficult/unpopular decisions 3. Listens to opinions when relevant 4. Is decisive when required 5. Consults as appropriate
3. Setting and Maintaining Standards	1. Establishes ground rules 2. Enforces ground rules 3. Leads by example
4. Using a Range of Styles	1. Selects style appropriate to circumstances 2. Exhibits use of range of styles
5. Showing Concern for the Group	1. Reach agreement on objectives 2. Encourage group to work together 3. Involve everyone 4. Control the group
6. Achieving the Task	1. Be successful in achieving objective 2. Work to the plan 3. Take the whole group along 4. Keep to time

7.3.2 Technical

UNDERPINNING FUNDAMENTALS	PERFORMANCE COMPONENTS

Posture	1 Ankles, knees and hips flexed
	2 Skeletally aligned so that you are supported by your bones
	3 Arm/hand carriage
	  - Arms away from the body
	  - Hands forward at about hip height
	4 Back rounded slightly
	5 Looking ahead/horizontal eye line

Balancing	1 Centred fore/aft 2 Appropriate lateral balance for task 3 Dynamic - balance is not static

> The above underpinning fundamentals must be used effectively during the performance of the following technical elements

TECHNICAL ELEMENTS	PERFORMANCE COMPONENTS
1 Straight Running	1 Balanced over the centre of each foot 2 Feet comfortably apart 3 Ankles, knees and hips flexed 4 Hands held forward and away from the body
2 Ploughing	1 Balance maintained whilst gliding 2 Use of plough to control speed 3 Ability to glide at constant speed
3 Plough Turning	1 Balance maintained throughout the turn 2 Increasing use of turn shape to control speed 3 Plough remains same shape throughout the turn 4 Use of perpendicular movements to apply and control pressure throughout the turn

TECHNICAL ELEMENTS	PERFORMANCE COMPONENTS
4 Plough-parallel	1 Balance maintained whilst steering 2 The inside ski is matched parallel after, in and before the fall line 3 Use of perpendicular movements to apply and control pressure throughout the turn 4 Skis continue steering throughout the turn 5 Speed increases as plough lessens
5 Basic Parallel	1 Balance maintained throughout turns 2 Feet and knees remain same distance apart throughout the turns 3 Tips and tails remain the same distance apart throughout the turns 4 Use of perpendicular movements to apply and control pressure throughout the turn 5 Turns are linked together 6 Pole plant is used to aid in the early part of the turn
6 Traversing	1 Balance is maintained 2 More natural weight will be on the downhill ski
7 Side Slipping	1 Skis remain across the fall line whilst slipping 2 Skis slide at constant speed
8 Swing to the Hill (Uphill Curve)	1 Balance maintained throughout 2 More pressure on the outside ski (downhill) 3 Skis steered from a steep traverse or fall line to a complete stop facing slightly back up the hill
9 Short Radius Turns (Performed on red runs)	1 Balance maintained throughout turns 2 Feet, knees, tips and tails remain the same distance apart throughout the turns 3 Use of dynamic movement from the ankles, knees and hips to control pressure throughout turns 4 Turns are linked and performed within a corridor showing control of speed and line 5 Pole plant is used at turn initiation to aid timing and coordination 6 Demonstration of good edge control to aid steering

TECHNICAL ELEMENTS	PERFORMANCE COMPONENTS
10 Long Radius Turns (Performed on red runs)	1 Balance maintained throughout turns 2 Feet, knees, tips and tails remain the same distance apart throughout the turns 3 Turns are linked and performed within a corridor showing control of speed and line 4 Demonstration of good edge control to aid steering
11 Carving (Performed on blue runs)	1 Balance maintained against the outside ski throughout turns 2 Turns are initiated by tilting the skis 3 Feet, knees, tips and tails remain the same distance apart throughout the turns 4 Edge control is maintained throughout the turns

Curves should have a beginning, middle and an end part.
Equal time and emphasis should be given to each part of the curve

7.3.3 Teaching

TEACHING ELEMENTS	PERFORMANCE COMPONENTS
1 Collects information	1 Starting standard of the group 2 Length of time available 3 Aspirations of the group
2 Produces a plan	1 Plans a ski session 2 Identifies key points for teaching 3 Identifies some development and/or corrective activities
3 Selects suitable teaching location	1 Location is safe 2 Location is suitable terrain for ability of class 3 Location is suitable for lesson content
4 Establishes lesson goals	1 Learning outcomes are relevant and are stated
5 Lesson structure and storyline	1 Lesson has a logical sequence 2 Activities are progressive 3 Activities are relevant to the learners

TEACHING ELEMENTS	PERFORMANCE COMPONENTS
6 Fault analysis	1 Faults are correctly identified
7 Fault correction	1 Appropriate correct activities are given
8 Improves performance	1 A measurable change takes place 2 Learning outcomes have been achieved 3 Learning outcomes have been measured
9 Gives feedback	1 Corrective feedback is given 2 Positive technical feedback is given 3 Motivational/encouraging feedback is given
10 Session review	1 Lesson is reviewed 2 Learning outcomes are achieved 3 Review is shared with others 4 Review outcome is recorded
11 Use of Mosston's teaching styles	1 Use of at least one of Mosston's Styles is evident

7.3.4 Presentation

PRESENTATION ELEMENTS	PERFORMANCE COMPONENTS
1 Content	1 Factually correct 2 Logically presented 3 Key points emphasised 4 Appropriate level of information 5 Related to Groups' experience
2 Personal presentation skills	1 Audible 2 Confidently presented 3 Enthusiastic 4 Positive use of body language
3 Method	1 Appropriate use of AV aids 2 Group involvement 3 Use of questions

	4 Feedback from the group
	5 Kept to time
4 Summary	1 Summary of key points
	2 Presentation objectives achieved

8 ASSESSMENT

8.1 ASSESSMENT STANDARDS

It is recognised that there are stages of learning which people progress through (see Chapter 2 for full details) Using the Fitts and Posner stages of learning model the Assessment Outcomes listed below have been graded either 1, 2 or 3. This refers to the "awareness" (Level 1), "practice" (Level 2) and "acquired" (Level 3) stages of learning and represent which stage you require to be performing at to be successful at assessment The following tables show the Assessment stages of learning for the required competencies of the Alpine Ski Leader. Candidates will be assessed on each of the Assessment Outcomes.

1 Leadership	Stage
1.1 Manages a group safely and effectively	3
1.2 Makes decisions	2
1.3 Sets and maintains standards	3
1.4 Uses a range of styles	2
1.5 Shows concern for the group	3
1.6 Achieves the task	3

2 Technical	Stage
2.1 Straight running	2
2.2 Ploughing	2
2.3 Plough turning	2
2.4 Plough parallel	2
2.5 Basic parallel	2
2.6 Traversing	1
2.7 Sideslipping	1
2.8 Swing to the Hill	1
2.9 Short Radius Turns (Performed on red runs)	2

	Stage
2.10 Long Radius Turns (Performed on red runs)	2
2.11 Carving (Performed on blue runs)	2
2.12 Posture	2
2.13 Balancing	2

3 Teaching	Stage
3.1 Collects information	2
3.2 Produces a plan	2
3.3 Selects suitable teaching location	2
3.4 Establishes lesson goals	2
3.5 Lesson structure and storyline	2
3.6 Fault analysis	2
3.7 Fault correction	2
3.8 Improves performance	2
3.9 Gives feedback	2
3.10 Reviews lesson effectiveness	2
3.11 Use of Mosston's teaching styles	2

4 Presentation	Stage
4.1 Content/accuracy	3
4.2 Personal presentation skills	3
4.3 Method	3
4.4 Summary	3

5 Mountain Skills	Stage
5.1 Knowledge of snowpack/structure	2
5.2 Knowledge of weather and its effects	2
5.3 Navigates effectively	3
5.4 Manages an accident/emergency situation	3
5.5 Carries out Risk Assessment	3

6 Personal Qualities	Stage
6.1 Punctuality	3
6.2 Appearance	3
6.3 Enthusiasm	3
6.4 Behaviour	3

teaching and learning

By the end of this section all candidates should be able to:

- State some learning principles
- Write a clear learning outcome
- Identify a range of teaching styles
- State how they might be used
- State how to give corrective feedback
- Describe different ways people learn
- Describe a Review Model
- Plan and review a lesson

BACKGROUND

Teaching has always been a key component of the Snowsport Scotland Alpine Ski Leader Award. When the award was originally designed, teachers, youth club leaders etc would solely organise ski trips, often for a weekend to Cairngorm, and they needed the tools to do everything. They organised the group, the transport, the accommodation (often a Youth Hostel), ski hire, did the teaching and once the group were ready, led them on ski runs. At night they would organise the cooking and evening activities then take the group back to the hill again the next day before driving the mini bus back home. Ski teaching was an integral part of the Alpine Ski Leader's role and even today, when most groups are taken abroad and access the local ski school, leaders still have an important teaching role.

Outwith ski school time, the Alpine Ski Leader can support the lesson only if he/she knows what stage of learning the pupil is at and knows what practices to give. In addition sometimes one or two pupils would benefit from individual tuition outwith ski school, and this too would be an effective way of making the trip more valuable for some pupils. The teaching component is designed for use with the Leaders' own group with whom they have travelled to resort with. It is always good practice to inform the Director of the local ski school that you will be working with your own pupils outwith ski school time.

In Scotland many teachers who hold the Alpine Ski Leader award still organise school ski trips in the way described above and many young people are taught to ski by them.

1 LEARNING PRINCIPLES

Before designing a learning experience for an individual or a group it is important to set a good learning environment. If the learning climate is right there is a better chance that learning will actually take place. It may take a few sessions to completely create such a learning environment, and it will be regularly challenged but focussing on it, and having perseverance, will pay dividends.

Take a moment and reflect on two situations which involved you learning something (one a successful learning experience and the other an unsuccessful learning experience).

If you were to turn the unsuccessful one into a successful one, what would you do?
Make a note of your top tips for creating a good learning experience before reading further.

Certain circumstances aid learning and some definitely do not. People do not learn when cold and wet or are too physically challenged or stressed.

Current research has shown that people learn best when:
• given time to **practise**
• it's **relevant** to their own situation and to the session outcomes
• they are **involved** in their own learning
• it is in a non threatening and supportive **climate**
• there is **enjoyment** and they have fun
• it is **learner** centred - at their own pace and in their own way
• their skills, knowledge and **experience** are respected
• they are encouraged to **self reflect** on their own behaviour
• they have **success** and their self esteem is raised

They are called Learning Principles.

Return to your two learning experiences and reflect firstly on the successful experience.
How many of the above learning principles were present?

From your note of your top tips for creating a good learning experience how many of the above learning principles were included?

The more of these learning principles which can be embraced the better chance the group will actually learn from the experience. Over a couple of days they can generally all be included and learning will become more likely for the learner.

The above model has the acronym "PRICELESS."

2 LEARNING OUTCOMES

"Inexperienced teachers coaches instructors and leaders teach material. Good teachers etc teach people" It is easy to prepare a lesson plan and follow it diligently delivering all the material in the time available. However, this alone does not guarantee that learning will take place.

Remember the little boy who attended all of the swimming lessons provided by his school. Following them his father took him to the local swimming pool. The boy wouldn't go into the water. His father asked "Why won't you go into the water? I thought you've been taught how to swim."
"I've been taught how to swim" the boy said, "but I just haven't learned how to do it yet!"

In order to be able to assess the effectiveness of any learning episode, clear learning outcomes require to be set. Learning outcomes are what you want the learner to be able to do as a result of your "lesson." The lesson should then be designed to ensure the learning outcome is met.

A learning outcome is a target for a learning episode!

- Deciding the outcome is harder than planning how to achieve it.
- Avoid woolly words like know, experience, understand etc.
- Limit the number of outcomes per session to a maximum of three or four.
- How will you know if the outcomes have been met?

An example of a learning outcome would be:
- "By the end of this session everyone will be able to DEMONSTRATE a snowplough turn."

This would be easy to assess by watching a performance. Either they can demonstrate it or not. If they can that learning outcome has been achieved. If not, then a review of the session should lead to identifying what the deliverer of that session needs to do in order for the learning outcome to be successfully achieved.

The learning outcome could be made more objective if it included a statement about turning to both sides.
- "By the end of this session everyone will be able to DEMONSTRATE a snowplough turn to the right and the left."

A further refinement might include a statement about the shape and size of the turn, or rhythmically linking several turns. There could be a statement about the quality of the performance such as posture. Initially the learning outcome should be quite simple and achievable. As performance improves and as your competence in writing learning outcomes develops clear, precise measurable outcomes will become easier to write. They should be designed to be appropriate and achievable for the group (or individual) in the location selected and in the time available.

It is best to avoid outcome verbs such as "to know" or "to understand". The outcome verb should be used to assess the success of the session and assessing if someone knows or understands something is difficult to measure.

Good outcome verbs include:
- list
- name
- identify
- describe
- explain
- prioritise
- demonstrate
- recall
- state
- report
- record
- select

teaching and learning

Using outcome verbs from the above list will aid designing a session and greatly assist your ability to assess its effectiveness. If the outcome is "by the end of this session pupils will be able to list what to carry on the hill for a days' skiing," at the end of the session you would expect to see a list (maybe on a flipchart) of what should be included.

If the outcome was "by the end of this session pupils will be able to identify or name parts of a ski and binding," at the end of the session you might point to parts of the ski and they should be able to name the parts correctly.

Time spent getting the precise learning outcome for a session will be time well invested. Do this thoroughly before determining the content of the session. Other parts of this book deal with content and teaching material and should be used to plan sessions.

3 TEACHING MODELS

3.1 MOSSTON
The aim of this section is to provide guidance on teaching "approaches" or "models". It should be recognised that an effective teacher adopts a flexible approach in common with an effective leader. The skilled teacher will use judgement and experience to decide how much responsibility to delegate to the learner and when the time is "right" to do so.

Whilst quality demonstrations, analysis of performance, selection of terrain, and good clear class management are vital skills to possess, so too is the ability to teach using various "approaches" or "styles" and to constantly evaluate the effectiveness of each style used with individuals and groups.

In all forms of modern education, the emphasis is increasingly on encouraging a more participative approach, with students becoming actively involved in their own learning. This section will focus on the work of a noted American Physical Educationalist, Muska Mosston. He has provided a model for studying teaching approaches which offers a useful framework for our purpose. This framework is known as "Mosston's Spectrum of Teaching Styles". Many national governing bodies of sport have now adopted Mosston's teaching styles as the basis for their coach education programmes.

One important area is how individuals learn. There are vast differences in how individuals learn, some are much more receptive to auditory signals, and others are predominately visual learners, whilst some learn most through active practice. Also, most individuals learn differently under different circumstances and at different rates. By being able to teach using a range of styles, leaders can greatly improve their chances of success with most individuals.

In his work Mosston makes it clear that each of his styles possesses key features and particular strengths and weaknesses. The spectrum is not presented as a hierarchy of style, and one is not necessarily better than any other. The best style is the one which will be most effective for the learners during any particular teaching episode.

Style "A" Command	Style "C" Reciprocal	Style "E" Inclusion	Style "G" Divergent	Style "I" Learner initiated
Style "B" Practice	Style "D" Self check	Style "F" Convergent	Style "H" Learners design	Style "J" Self teaching

The styles, up to Learner's Design, are the ones most likely to be used and they are the ones described below.

Style A - "Command Style"
In this style, the teacher directs the members of his/her class in all their actions; a clear comparison being possible with a sergeant major controlling a group of recruits on a barracks square.

Key Features of the Command Style are:
To learn to perform a task accurately and efficiently. It provides for teacher control and learner compliance. The learner does not take any active decisions except consenting to take part.

Implications
- Subject matter is fixed, a single standard to be followed.
- The teacher's demonstration of the skill establishes the model to be copied.
- The teacher's commands must be obeyed with great care in performance.
- The teacher's decisions cannot be questioned.
- Individual differences in the abilities of learners cannot be taken into consideration.

Use
- Starting off with a new group
- Coping with an unforeseen crisis
- Leading in hazardous positions on, for example, a steep slope

teaching and learning

Style B - "Practice Style"

This style enables the teacher to provide the class with a model of performance, probably by demonstration, which the student then tries, with repetition, more or less at their own pace. It is perhaps the style of teaching most frequently employed by teachers of physical activities particularly when introducing a new technique.

Key Features of the Practice Style are:

It provides for near maximum opportunity to practise the task at hand and to receive feedback individually and privately.

Implications

- Students learn to make certain (not all) decisions about performance and to accept the consequences of those decisions.
- They learn to perform tasks within constraints of time and space.
- They learn to accept private and individual feedback.

Use:

Plough parallel matching skis:-
- Smoothly
- In fall line
- Before fall line

Style C - "Reciprocal Style

In this style the teacher divides the class into twos or threes, whose members work together as "performer" and "observer" in turn, providing each other with immediate feedback according to clear criteria provided by the teacher.

Key Features of the Reciprocal Style are:

By working co-operatively, partners provide each other with immediate, one-to-one feedback. Evaluations of the performance of a skill/activity are shifted from teacher to learner who observes a partner's performance and also provides feedback on the basis of criteria laid down by the teacher.

Implications
- This style promotes a new kind of relationship among learners.
- Patience and tolerance are developed and exhibited.
- Reciprocation of giving and receiving feedback is developed and exhibited.
- Precision in offering feedback by criteria is developed.
- Learning the task itself is facilitated due to immediate feedback from the partner.
- The teacher can stand back and monitor the work of the observers as well as the developments of the whole group.

Use:
- Straight running
- Various activities when posture is in focus

Style D - "Self-Check Style"
Whilst operating in this style, the teacher enables the class or group to work individually to analyse and reflect upon their own performance. However, the correct direction and guidelines are still provided by the teacher.

Key Features of the self-check style are:
The self-check style provides opportunities for self-assessment. By a further shift in decision making, a situation is created in which the learners' skills in analysing performance are enhanced, and they are required to apply those skills to analyse their own performance rather than that of a learning partner.

Implications
- Learners expand their experience in working privately.
- They learn to "feel" and "sense" their own performance.
- They learn to use criteria to improve their own performance.
- They learn to be honest and objective about their own performance.
- They learn about discrepancies and their own limitations.

- They learn to be more independent of the teacher as the sole source of feedback.
- There is more individualising than in previous styles. Learners make individual decisions about themselves both in the "performance" and "reflective" phase.

Use:
- Ploughing to stop at a point
- Leaving clear marks whilst carving on good snow
- Smooth matching of skis whilst plough paralleling

Style E - "Inclusion Style"

In this style learners are again allowed to operate individually, but are provided with more opportunities for selecting the level at which they attempt a particular activity; more or less demanding according to choice.

Key Features of the Inclusion Style are:

The Inclusion Style provides the opportunity for each learner to be included in the task at hand. In each of the styles identified so far, the task had been thought of in terms of a single standard and no consideration has been given to individual differences amongst learners. Up to this point, the teacher has the opportunity to alter the nature of the feedback in accordance with the learners' performance but this does not alter the fact that learners have been working towards a teacher-determined level of performance. Style E addresses this problem which is of crucial importance to all teachers.

Implications

- The learner is given the opportunity to select a standard that suits his/her abilities.
- The teacher's main task is to ensure that there is a sufficient range of options available.
- Opportunity is provided to choose the standard of performance where success can be "guaranteed".
- There is the opportunity to take a step backward in order to succeed in the activity.
- There are options to move on if one wishes to do so.
- Promotes learning of self-assessment and deals with the (frequent) discrepancy between aspiration and reality.

Use:
- Ploughing to a stop in stopping zone
- Plough turning using a forest of poles

Style F - "Guided Discovery" (Convergent Style)

Here, the success of the style rests on the effectiveness of the teacher in asking questions of the learner or learners. The questions may be posed verbally or by setting problems, but should result in the learners reaching a similar conclusion to the teacher, "converging" in their thinking.

Key Features of the Guided Discovery Style are:

None of the styles identified so far have made significant demands of learners in terms of their ability to understand and think more deeply about performance, rather they have been concerned with reproduction of knowledge as given by the teacher. To develop situations wherein learners have a different relationship to that knowledge, Mosston claims that learners have to go beyond the discovery threshold (F and G). The first of two styles which takes learners beyond this discovery threshold is based on the notion of "guided discovery" and the process of CONVERGENT THINKING.

Performance:

teacher presents a situation to create a thinking process in the learner which, when resolved, becomes subject matter (e.g. "Which part of a turn do you extend and which part do you flex"?)

Evaluation:

when feedback information is fundamental to the task, the learner can evaluate their own responses; otherwise the teacher provides the feedback.

Style F is dependant on the teacher's skill in asking appropriate questions, in sequence, during the performance phase.

Implications

- Develops a precise relationship between the learner's response and the stimulus (questions presented by the teacher).
- Develops a relationship between the teacher and the learners which is based on discovery by a learner (this is fundamentally different from the stimulus-response relationship that occurs in the Command Style A).
- Develops sequential discovery skills that logically lead to the discovery of a concept.
- Develops the patience (in both teacher and learner) required during the discovery process.

Use:

- Use of flexion and extension through a turn
- Finding a home base

Style G - "Divergent Style"

While the teacher still poses the question or sets the problem in this style, in contrast with the previous (Convergent) style, the answer or answers may be varied and unexpected. In others words, the learner is required to both understand more and be more creative than previously.

teaching and learning

Key Features of the Divergent Style are:
This style of teaching is based on the process of divergent thinking. The shift in decision making which identifies this style of teaching is outlined as:

Performance:
learners create subject matter by discovering alternative solutions to questions posed by the teacher (e.g. working as a formation ski team)

Evaluation:
depending on subject matter, learner verifies own solutions or receives feedback from the teacher

This style requires the teacher to consider and use something called the "reduction process", which can be defined as, "the successive use of criteria to reduce a given number of solutions". For example, is a particular day's planned route possible for a given group given the constraints of fitness, terrain, weather, time of year, equipment, group skill etc? Is it feasible with the time available? Is it the "best" and most rewarding route for the group?

Implications
- To tap the thinking capacities of the teacher in designing problems in a given subject matter area.
- To tap the thinking capacities of the learners in discovering multiple solutions to any given problem.
- To develop insight into the nature of the activity and discover possible variations.
- To reach the level of effective security which "permits" the teacher and the learner to go beyond accepted responses, i.e.to go beyond the conventional.
- To develop the ability to confirm solutions and test them in context.

Use:
- Synchro skiing
- Planning a day's route

Style H - "Learner Designed Programme"

Although the teacher may still prescribe the general area of enquiry for the learner or learners, it would be up to the learners to identify the specific problem to be solved or design the programme to be followed. Perhaps, if they wish, they could call upon the teacher for advice, guidance or even direct instruction.

This style requires the learner to use the skill and understanding developed earlier, and apply them in a context in which work is undertaken much more independently of the teacher. In style H the learner identifies the questions or problems prescribed by the teacher. This style, which can only be followed over a series of episodes, is dependant on the learner having a sound understanding of the subject matter. Only then can the learner identify relevant questions in a highly disciplined manner and thus avoid the situation in which "anything goes".

Style H provides opportunities for students to develop initiative and be guided and reminded, if necessary, during the progress of a self-motivated project. The main limitation is that the project has to be undertaken within the parameters of the teacher's knowledge, conditions, time etc.

Use:
- Use of pressure
- Creating more grippy turns

SUMMARY

Styles and their use have to be judged on how appropriate they are. Decisions about their suitability can only be made by the teacher whilst taking into account:

- Maturity of the learner
- Nature of the activity (complexity, danger element)
- Confidence/competence of the teacher

Expectations of the learner in terms of how the teacher will operate are a significant factor in any teacher/learner situation. It is important, therefore, that the respective roles are clarified before any teaching episode begins and re-enforced as the episode progresses.

Research has shown that Teachers who use a spectrum of styles display the following qualities:
- Exhibit flexibility in different use of styles
- Give more individual attention to students
- Spend less time dominating discussions

teaching and learning

Use time more efficiently, evidenced by:
- students pay more attention
- more time is spent on work
- less time is spent on distractions
- less time is spent on discipline
- more subject matter is taught

And "Spectrum" Students show corresponding characteristics:
- greater flexibility in coping with learning demands
- more independence and responsibility
- posses a clearer idea of tasks and roles

Helping people to learn can be particularly challenging, and carrying out this role effectively is vital. Initially there is likely to be the desire to operate in a "command" style of teaching. As confidence and experience grow, the leader is likely to experiment with the ranges of "styles" outlined in this section. Such experimentation is normal and should be regularly evaluated for effectiveness. Eventually, the complete range of styles should be well within the repertoire of skills which the effective leader can employ. As more and more responsibility is undertaken by group members and as their skills develop, the leader must avoid "holding on" and recognise that such a development can be considered the result of effective instruction.

3.2 EDICT

Another model which is simple and useful for setting up a lesson, taken from an early 1970's BCU canoe coaching manual, is EDICT. It has been modified slightly over the years but the original model is still useful and easy to use.

In this model the sequence for teaching a skill is:
- Explanation
- Demonstration
- Imitation
- Correction
- Trials

a) Explanation:
it should be concise and simple. The important points should be emphasised and points which are not strictly necessary omitted. A thorough knowledge of the skill to be taught and the learner's ability to learn it are important parts. The explanation whilst concise must be explained in suitable logical steps.

b) Demonstration:
This must be to the correct standard and clear for the learners to see. (Research has shown that it is best to demonstrate in silence)

c) Imitation:
Let the group try it for themselves

d) Correction:
Any faults must be corrected.

e) Trials:
the practice should continue until improvement is made.

This simple model will be easily recognised. It is easy to use and is a very successful model especially for someone inexperienced in teaching. If uncertain about using Mosston's styles this provides a useful model to get started.

4 FEEDBACK

During a session, feedback to the learner on his/her performance is vital. In the event of something not working well what the learner wants to know is what to do to make it better. Most people simply state what was wrong. A much more effective way of giving feedback is initially to praises the good parts of the performance then give corrective feedback.

Two key sentences should be used. The first starts
"What I liked about your performance was.............................."
and the second begins with
"What would make it even better would be........................"

The value of the first sentence is that it praises the learner, confirms what is good and gets his/her attention. The second sentence is very important in that it should give the learner information which can immediately be used to improve to improve their next attempt.

E.g." What I liked about your snowplough turn was your good posture looking ahead and holding your hands in a good position. What was also good was that you maintained a constant speed."
"What would make it even better would be to keep the wedge shape the same size throughout the turn by rotating both legs."

Get these two key sentences into your feedback repertoire. Make it a habit to give feedback in this way and it will greatly aid setting a good learning climate as well as helping the learner to improve.

Before giving feedback it is useful to consider which part of a performance it is which requires most attention. The idea of using the following four quadrants was introduced to Scottish sport by a visiting East German Volleyball Coach, Horst Baacke. He introduced the concept of looking at a performance and then deciding which area needed development. The four key areas are;

TECHNICAL	TACTICAL
PHYSICAL	PSYCHOLOGICAL

This started out as the Tactical Periodization Method which was developed by Vitor Frade (Professor at the Sports Uni in Porto) to find the best way to train players in order for them to reach their potential. The method is based around 4 different movements in football and four key elements, namely, PHYSICAL, TECHNICAL, TACTICAL and PSYCHOLOGICAL.

One of Frade's theories was that there is no use in doing a purely fitness based training session as it will only work on the Physical and Psychological elements of a player. All four elements must be included in each drill which organises the team for one of the four movements of the game. This training method was adapted by Baacke and used to analyse performance of players. Whilst this was introduced as a volleyball coaching technique, volleyball coaches who were also involved in other sports found they were able to use it successfully in a range of coaching situations. Some Governing Bodies of Sport make use of it in their coach education programmes as it is a transferrable model.

When looking at a performance, instead of rushing in with only a technical feedback it is useful to fully reflect on what is hindering the perfect performance. It might be found in one of the other three areas and your feedback should reflect this. It may take some time to develop expertise and confidence in this way of analysing performance. Initially the challenge of spotting the fault and diagnosing the cause and then to be able to provide corrective feedback will be challenging enough. However it is worth remembering that the solution might not be a technical one.

5 LEARNING

5.1 LEARNING STAGES

Before focussing on learning styles it is useful to remember that learning takes place at different rates. All learners go through a process of stages which have been identified by Fitts and Posner, and described by them as "learning stages".

At the start of a new learning experience we are all "unconscious incompetents". In other words "we don't know what we don't know". Once something new is explained or a demonstration given we become "conscious competent" or we know what it is but we don't quite know how to do it yet. As practice begins we have some successes which is the "conscious competence" stage and finally the new skill can be performed under any conditions and in any circumstances without thinking about it - "unconscious competence".

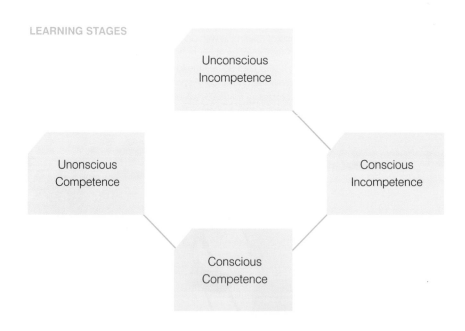

LEARNING STAGES

Unconscious Incompetence

Conscious Incompetence

Conscious Competence

Unonscious Competence

These stages of learning are known as "Awareness", "Practice" and "Acquired". During any training course candidates will be exposed to many learning opportunities and will be constantly moving around the stages of learning. People learn in different ways as well as at different rates.

Practice makes permanent and bad habits are difficult to change. Therefore good practice should always be the target when practising skills.

On conclusion of your course, some skills will require to be at the acquired phase whilst others can be at the practice phase. In the section on assessment standards in chapter 1, these learning stages have been used: awareness is 1, practice is 2 and acquired is 3.

LEARNING STAGES

I don't know what I dont know

Acquired Phase

Awareness Phase

Practice Phase

5.2 LEARNING STYLES

Dr Peter Honey and Alan Mumford (1986) developed a learning styles questionnaire, based on Kolb and others' work, to measure how people learn, to identify their learning strengths, to encourage individuals to develop their learning potential and report on how they can improve their learning style. They clarified the four main learning styles as:

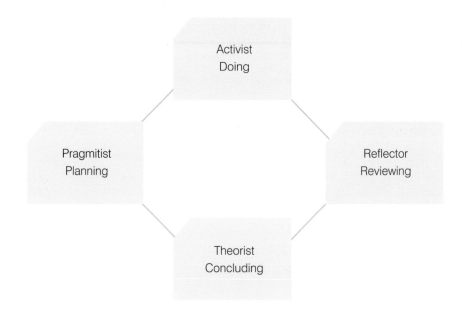

As in the case of Kolb's theory, people may not be fully effective learners in all stages of the learning cycle. The purpose of Honey & Mumford's work was to identify the stage(s) at which your learning is most effective i.e. your preferred learning style.

The four learning preferences described as follows:

Activist

If you're an activist you like involving yourself fully in new experiences. You'll try anything once, in an open-minded way. You enjoy the here and now, and like 'getting stuck into' immediate problems, busily looking for solutions by brainstorming. You're good at short-term crisis fire-fighting. You don't like caution or boredom and are not keen on having to implement or consolidate your ideas, preferring to look for the excitement of a new challenge. Your sociable but like to be the centre of attention.

Theorist

You prefer to think problems through in a logical step-by-step way. You like analysing and integrating ideas into complex but coherent theories. You are something of a perfectionist seeking to create tidy, rational systems. You feel most comfortable working with theoretical models, basic assumptions and principles. You tend to be detached and objective. You are very uncomfortable with ambiguity or subjectivity. You are intolerant of uncertainty or lateral thinking, in fact anything that doesn't fit into your theoretical framework.

Reflector

You tend to be cautious and thoughtful, liking to collect and analyse as much data as possible, before coming to a decision. You like to 'sleep on it'. You keep a low profile in discussions, preferring to observe and listen to others, seeing in which direction the discussion is going before making your own contributions.

Pragmatist

You are enthusiastic about trying out new theories and techniques in practice. You prefer to get on with things, acting quickly and confidently with ideas that you like. You get frustrated with 'beating about the bush' or long-winded, open-ended discussions. You are thoroughly practical, enjoy challenges and solving problems, and are always looking for better ways of doing things. Your view is 'if it works its good'.

When helping people to learn account has to be taken of their learning preferences. The table below shows appropriate delivery styles to suit learning preferences.

	Delivery style preferences	Learning preferences
ACTIVISTS:	• games • small group discussions • outdoor activities • role-plays • teaching others	• think out loud • quick to take part • willing to answer questions
REFLECTORS:	• e-learning • reviews • lectures/presentations • observing role-plays • reading • self-study	• quiet, wants time to think • thinks first, speaks later

teaching and learning

THEORISTS:	• analysing • tasks with right answers • lectures/presentations • self-study • solo exercises	• ask 'why?' • need to know the theory first
PRAGMATISTS:	• discussions about problems • small group discussions • group tasks • problem solving tasks • projects	• need to see the relevance • if it works, will do it

In the following picture everyone is being taught the same thing by the Leader in the purple suit. The learners are all approaching the task differently according to their own learning preferences.

When reviewing a lesson after checking that the learning outcomes have been achieved reflect on those who were less successful in the group. If the lesson was not successful for a small number, you should consider whether or not their preferred learning style was accommodated in that session?

5.3 RETENTION RATE

Whether you have responsibility to set the direction for the staff development program or have the day-to-day responsibility for educating, understanding and utilizing the learning pyramid can improve individual skill development and retention. The learning pyramid provides information on the average learning retention rates based on the delivery method. Bear this in mind when attempting to help someone to learn. Doing and Teaching will aid retention of information. The "Reciprocal" method of teaching has much to commend it if the learners are mature enough to use it. During your Alpine Ski Leader course you should expect to be DOING and TEACHING for much of the time to give you the best chance of retaining as much information from your course as possible.

The following research model confirms why this approach is taken.

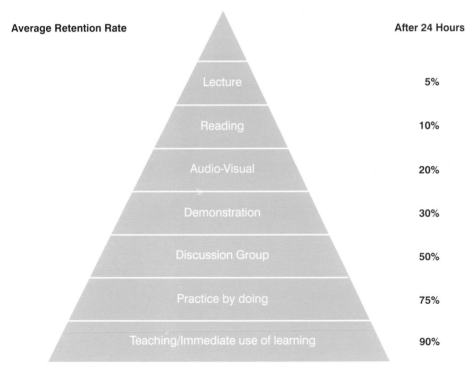

Average Retention Rate	After 24 Hours
Lecture	5%
Reading	10%
Audio-Visual	20%
Demonstration	30%
Discussion Group	50%
Practice by doing	75%
Teaching/Immediate use of learning	90%

Most effective learning comes from people doing it for themselves
Least effective learning comes from simply being told
(Source: National Training Laboratories, Bethel, Maine)

teaching and learning

5.4 REVIEWING

A useful model to aid learning is the Kolb Cycle of Experiential Learning. The Kolb cycle has four stages and it cycle and can be joined at any stage. Where a student picks up the Kolb Cycle will depend on the favoured learning style of the student involved (see Learning Styles in Para 5.2).

Stage 1 - Concrete Experience (DO)
We do something. These learning experiences are those gained real situations or from simulations of real situations.

Stage 2 - Reflective Observation (REVIEW)
We think about the experience and try to make sense of it. This reflection should be ordered and as objective as possible.

Stage 3 - Abstract Conceptualisation (LEARN)
We look for "rules" to apply to similar situations. At this stage the learner would try to apply theory to the concrete experience and see if their own experience supports the theory or not.

Stage 4 - Planning Active Experimentation (APPLY)
We try out our learned "rules" in a similar situation to see if they have the same results. If they do, we have learned.

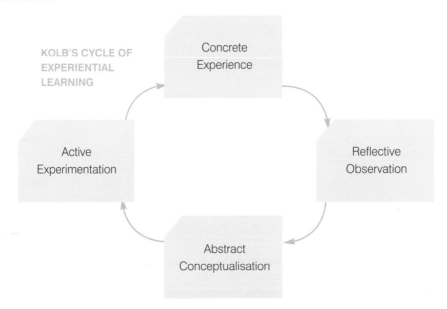

A key part of this model is the review stage. Asking appropriate open questions will help the review process.

At the end of a practice the teacher often asks the learner:
"How did that go?" or "how was that this time".

This opens the door for the answer:
"OK"

This is not a review nor will it reveal anything.
It is always useful to consider what you really want the learner to do when asking a question.
It is always good to get the learner to think.

A reviewer might ask:
"What did you do to make that work" or "what did you do differently from last time?"

During your ASL course you will be involved in reviewing your sessions and others' sessions. A Review Model will be used for that process. This model is used when training Tutors and is particularly good at getting both the deliverer of a session and the recipients to think and reflect. Thinking and reflecting aids learning.

teaching and learning

Review Model

Stages	Sample statement/questions
R re-assure and re-Integrate	Thank you, I really liked the way you... It was great the way you You did really well when ...
E establish focus on Objectives/goals	What did you want to achieve yourself? What was your personal goal? What did you want the group to be able to achieve at the end (i.e. competence)?
V visit through questions • 'What went well? • For what reason?'	In trying to achieve your goals, what went well? What else went well? What about...., how did that go?
• 'What went less well? • For what reason?'	If you had a chance to do it again, what would you do differently? What didn't go to plan? What were you less happy about?
I invite group to contribute in a structured way and add your own input	What else did you think xx did well? What about....? How else ....? How could that have been achieved?
E emphasise and summarise key points raised	Lots of useful things there - let me try to summarise them for you... (briefly pick out the key issues)
W 'what have you learnt?' and 'what will you now do?'	Ask the deliverer these questions and try to nail precisely what they will do with what they have learnt to change their delivery in the future

6 SESSION PLANNING

Not everyone is comfortable preparing a lesson on a predetermined planning sheet. What is delivered and how effective learning takes place is much more important. However in order to ensure a structured and progressive approach it is useful to plan a lesson in detail especially during formative teaching days. A Session Planning sheet will be used on your training course. (see exemplar on pages 57 & 58)

Page 1 asks all of the important lesson planning questions such as:
• Setting the main session goal
• Clearly stating the learning outcomes
• Determining the session content
• Deciding on the delivery style
• Listing relevant coaching points likely to be required
• Ensuring you can assess the outcomes

Page 2 of the session planning sheet assists with the evaluation of the lesson. It asks about:
- Assessing if learning took place by revisiting all of the learning outcomes (did the final task generate evidence)
- Improving parts of the session which could be made better (which could include reflection on consideration being given to learning styles)
- Preparation of an action plan for the next time

Some general questions to ask yourself following every session you deliver.
- What did you do to make the session effective?
- How do you know you achieved your outcomes/goals?
- If you were starting again would you change anything?
- How did you ensure that learning took place?
- What did you do to motivate the class to return for the next session
- What did you do to ensure everyone was full engaged?
- If time was a problem what would you jettison?

Make plans for the range of sessions you are likely to have to deliver. Build up a bank of sessions. Review them after delivery and keep refining them based on your experiences delivering them and you will develop a good range of sessions likely to be able to assist learners at all stages of their development. It does take some time to become competent in this area, especially if you are not teaching skiing on a regular and frequent basis. Eventually, as your experience develops, you will be able to deliver an appropriate session from the toolkit of activities and practices you carry around inside your head. The time invested in planning sessions early in your ski teaching career will pay dividends in the long run.

teaching and learning

Snowsport Scotland   **Sample Session Plan**

Session Topic *Snowplough Turning*	Date *01/04/09*	Time *0930 – noon*	Venue *Ptarmigan Bowl Cairngorm*

Client: *Third year school pupils (Mixed Class)*   No in class: *10*

Learning outcomes - by the end of this session class members will be able to:
- *Demonstrate a plough turn to the right and to the left*
- *Demonstrate 2 – 4 linked plough turns*
- *Demonstrate good balance throughout the manoeuvre*
- *Keep the plough shape constant throughout*

Safety Considerations: *Gentle slope with good run out*   Other:
                           Good space and wide area

Risk Assessment: *Preparatory sessions mean that group is ready for this session. Area wide and not busy. Snow conditions are good with new grippy snow just pisted.*

Equipment/resources required: *Marker cones/buttons, Ski poles & Cards for reciprocal session*

Timing	Session Content	Teaching Style
30mins	*Warm up* *Recap on last session – ploughing (controlling speed)* *Practice*	*Command*
30mins	*Plough turn to one side (to a stop)* *then Plough turn to other side (to a stop*	*EDICT* *Reciprocal*
20mins	*Link 2 – 4 turns (close to the fall line to begin with)*	*Command*
20mins	*Use drills with a 2 – 4 turn course (under gate/step over pole/ catch glove etc).*	*Practice*
20 mns	*Forest of poles*	*Practice and Inclusion*
10mns	*Dual slalom*	*Command*

Coaching points:
1 *Balance maintained whilst steering*
2 *Increasing use of turn shape to control speed*
3 *Plough remains same shape/size throughout the turn by rotating both legs*
4 *Use of vertical movements to apply and control pressure throughout the turn*

Sample Session Evaluation

Numbers expected; 10	Numbers participated; 9
Equipment planned *Marker cones / buttons* *Ski poles* *Cards for reciprocal session*	Equipment used *Ski poles* *Cards for reciprocal session*

How well was each learning outcome achieved?: *They were all achieved but not all to the same standard. Most of the group achieved them pretty well but a couple need more practice time.*

How do you know?: *I used the LO's to check and I observed everyone's performance.*

Consider the following; if NO note the reason below	YES	NO
1. Did everyone enjoy himself or herself?	√	
2. Did learning take place?	√	
3 Did you check using the learning outcome verb?	√	
4. Was your preparation thorough enough?		√
5. Did you follow the session as planned?	√	
6. Did you keep to the planned timings?		√
7. Did all of your activities work?	√	
8. Did the group respond positively to your activities?	√	
9. Did you encourage and motivate?	√	
10. Were the demonstrations effective?	√	
11. Was corrective feedback used?	√	
12. Would you have enjoyed being in that session?	√	
13. Did the group give you positive feedback?	√	

For all the NO answers, write what you will do to turn them around.

1. I planned for an even number but only had 9. This caused me to have to make quick adjustments to the partner activities I had planned. I joined in to make up a pair but then couldn't watch the others practicing. I need to plan for working in threes as well.

2. I needed to reset the marker cones as the slope was too shallow and I placed the markers too close together. I need to trial practices on the space I have so that I can be sure they will always help learning to take place.

Goals for next session

1. Keep setting good learning outcomes and assess success by using them

2. Overall I kept to time but some of the parts were different to the timings stated. I think this was OK as groups will progress at different stages anyway. I will not deliberately stick to the stated time for each activity.

3. I need to prepare to include activities for groups of three as well as two

4. I need to practice setting up drills and practices by trialing different spacing and using different slope angles so that they will always work.

Snowsport Scotland   **Sample Session Plan**

Session Topic		Date	Time	Venue

Client: No in class:

Learning outcomes - by the end of this session class members will be able to:

Safety Considerations: Other:

Risk Assessment:

Equipment/resources required:

Timing	Session Content	Teaching Style

Coaching points:

teaching and learning

Sample Session Evaluation

Numbers expected;   Numbers participated;

Equipment planned   Equipment used

How well was each learning outcome achieved?:

How do you know?:

Consider the following; if NO note the reason below	YES	NO
1. Did everyone enjoy himself or herself?		
2. Did learning take place?		
3 Did you check using the learning outcome verb?		
4. Was your preparation thorough enough?		
5. Did you follow the session as planned?		
6. Did you keep to the planned timings?		
7. Did all of your activities work?		
8. Did the group respond positively to your activities?		
9. Did you encourage and motivate?		
10. Were the demonstrations effective?		
11. Was corrective feedback used?		
12. Would you have enjoyed being in that session?		
13. Did the group give you positive feedback?		

For all the NO answers, write what you will do to turn them around.

Goals for next session

7 SUMMARY OF TEACHING

To give learners the best possible chance of learning you must take account of the following steps:

- Set the best learning climate (this process will require to permeate all sessions)
- Decide on the topic to be taught
- Establish clear learning outcomes
- Construct a lesson with appropriate content which will aid learning (need to have rather than nice to have content)
- Consider the range of learning styles in the class/group
- Decide on teaching styles required to aid learning
- Set learning outcome assessments

technical

By the end of this section all candidates should be able to:
- Describe the key aspects of the Skiing Fundamentals
- Outline the key steps from beginner skier to parallel skier
- Explain the skiing activities described in this section
- Use the ASL Skills Activity Card format to develop further activities

Introduction to Technical Skiing Chapter

This chapter is divided into three sections; Skiing Fundamentals, Progression from Beginner to Parallel and Skiing Activities. Before you can develop either your own performance or that of others it is essential that you understand how skiing works hence the need to understand the skiing fundamentals. These fundamentals can then be applied to the progression that all skiers move through from beginner to parallel. And finally with this knowledge of how skiers develop through the progression there is a very useful section with examples of activities that you the alpine ski leader can use with the groups that you are leading.

1) Skiing Fundamentals

Introduction

All sports are based around fundamentals which underpin efficient and effective performance. Understanding these fundamentals and how they effect performance is essential for both skiers and ski leaders if you are to get the maximum enjoyment from the sport. The first part of this technical chapter focuses on these fundamentals and looks more closely at three key areas; **Control** (of speed & direction), **Movements & Balancing** and **Steering**. A sound knowledge of these fundamentals will allow, you, the alpine ski leader to better understand how skiing works right through from complete beginner to parallel and beyond.

1.1 Control (of speed & direction)

Without wanting to state the obvious "controlling your speed & direction" is essential for all skiers. While there are a number of ways in which you can control your speed and direction the key elements that you need to understand are **skidding** (brushing off speed as you steer your skis around the curve), **curve length** (how far your skis travel past the fall line) and **corridors** (the shape of turns you make in any given corridor).

Skidding your skis is about blending the **three** steering elements together to produce a rounded curve at slower speeds. The path of a skidded ski will involve the tail washing out to the side as the tip moves to the inside (created by pivoting under your foot). Conversely a ski can be said to be carved when the path of the tip and the tail are the same. However a key point here is that there is a big difference in the "quality" of skidding as this has a direct effect on the quality of curve that you produce.

Diagram 1
(the path of a skidded ski)

Many people advocate that skidding is bad! This is a misconception as skidding is an essential skill if you want to be able to effectively ski the whole mountain. There is however such a thing as "good skidding" and "bad skidding". The difference between the two was summed up recently by an instructor who was participating in a staff training session that I was running when he said PNP. This simply stands for "Pivot not Push".

Side slipping is an essential component for developing control, balance and more importantly good skidding. Many skiers struggle once a slope becomes icy and the common stated solution is that "I need to get more edge". However what often happens is that the skier edges the skis by leaning the whole body into the hill and consequently loses balance and control as the skis slide out from underneath them (bad skidding). By developing your side slipping skills you learn to slide and therefore skid in balance. This will allow you to more easily pivot from under your foot and then blend in appropriate edge control by tilting the skis onto their edges using a gentle rolling of the feet towards the hill. So the next time you come across an icy slope, edge less initially so that you maintain balance and slide in control. Then think about edging from the feet up!

Your **curve length** is simply how far you travel around the arc, past the fall line, before releasing from that turn. The phrase "finish your turn" is often used by instructors but not always understood by the learner! The gradient will have a big impact on how much you need to finish your turns. If you release too early on steeper terrain then your speed will increase. Conversely if you release too late on moderate terrain then your flow down the mountain will be interrupted as you lose too much speed.

Skiing **corridors** is about making different turn shapes within a defined corridor. Using a combination of skidding and curve length you will be able to make a variety of turn shapes on different gradients within different corridors widths.

The ideal way to measure your success at skiing a consistent corridor is to look back at your tracks on a nice powder day. The goal should be to leave perfect "S" shaped tracks in the snow. However powder days are few and far between so skiing piste machine widths on a groomed slope or using the edge of the piste to define one wall of a corridor are more practical ways to achieve this. Of course you can also set out a corridor using poles or markers.

Skiing corridors - Tracks on a nice powder day

1.2 Movements & Balancing

The movements that you make affect your balance in either a positive or negative way! To help you understand good and bad movements it is useful to look at the ways that you can move. In other words there are three planes of movement - lateral, vertical and fore/aft, plus rotary movements that happen about an axis.

Lateral movement is more simply described as "side to side". You can move or lean your whole body to the inside of a turn and this is often referred to as **inclination** and allows you to edge your skis at the top of your turns. However, if you lean the body too far or too quickly to the inside (**banking**), you will end up either supported on your inside ski or worse still falling over.

As the turn shape develops you need to maintain control of your skis and keep effective balance against the outer ski of the turn. The hip, knee and ankle are all used to control the turn with the upper body reacting appropriately (**angulation**) to help maintain balance.

Vertical movements essentially involve extension and flexion of the legs. The execution of this requires a great deal of practice so that you learn to extend and flex the ankles, knees and hips in unison while maintaining a centred position. Timing is also important as this greatly effects how you control your skis. For example a quick extension will result in the skis being un-weighted at the end of the movement. Conversely, a gradual extension will help to maintain the control and grip of your skis against the snow.

Fore/aft movements are generally fairly subtle and are used to keep the skis working from tip to tail. These movements become more obvious when skiing bumps as the change in terrain requires fore/aft adjustment to help achieve and maintain ski to snow contact.

Breaking movements down into three planes does in one sense help to simplify how you move, however it is important to understand that in a skilful skiing performance you combine these planes of movement. You do not simply move "up and down" to make your turns but rather combine lateral and vertical movements e.g. at the start of the new turn, as the hips move to the inside of the curve you extend your legs to apply pressure to your skis.

Rotary movements (about an axis) in layman's terms means "turning" and this could involve any part of the body. If for example I were to do a 360° spin, this would involve rotating the whole body. However, in general, when referring to rotary movements we are talking about turning our legs within our hip socket. You use this movement so that you can pivot your feet/skis (independently of the upper body) and this is an essential component for steering your skis which is described in more detail later is this chapter.

Appropriate movements aid effective **balancing**. The reason for the term "balancing" rather than balance is to highlight that the process of balancing is not static. To maintain balance you must continually make little adjustments. To highlight this point try standing on one foot and notice how you make subtle little movements in order to stay balanced. If you want to emphasise this even more then close your eyes.

Maintaining balance, while skiing is more complex than balancing while standing still. Balance in motion can be broken down into two distinct areas; Fore/aft (backwards & forwards) and lateral (side to side).

As you turn your skis you must maintain a relatively "centred" position so that you are stacked and balanced over your feet. Good **fore/aft balance** is achieved when you are supported by your bones through good skeletal alignment. To achieve this you need even flexion of your ankles, knees and hips. For example too much flexion in the knees and hips without ankle flex will quickly lead to very tired muscles.

technical

Lateral balance can easily be compared to a cyclist going round a corner. If he/she leans the bicycle too far over in relation to the speed that they are travelling then they will fall over. In skiing, you tilt your skis and allow your body to lean to the inside of the turn. However, you must do this accurately so that you maintain effective balance against the outer ski of the turn. If you want to test your skills at balancing then try turning using only the outer ski of the turn. This is best done initially on easier terrain. Try to keep your outer ski carving cleanly while keeping the inner ski lifted off the snow. You can get instant feedback (intrinsic) from this drill as to how well you are balancing both fore/aft and laterally. If your fore/aft balance is good then the lifted ski should be fairly level (not higher at the tip or tail!). And if your lateral balance is good you should be able to keep the inner ski lifted for the entire turn without any falling to the inside! This particular activity is covered in the third part of this chapter and is one of the "black - beyond parallel" activities.

1.3 Steering

I often describe skiing to my students in a very simplified way; i.e., there are just three things that you can do to your skis; Stand on them (pressure), tilt them (edging) and pivot them (rotation). However the complex part of this involves **blending** these three elements together. Lets' take a look at each of these elements. **Pressure control** is often an area that causes confusion. As soon as you stand on a ski, you put weight on it and therefore exert some pressure. What you need to know is how to use pressure control within a turn and what effect gravity has on your skis. So when do you apply pressure to influence the turn and when do you control and manage pressure that is already there?

Diagram 2
(Applying & Managing Pressure)

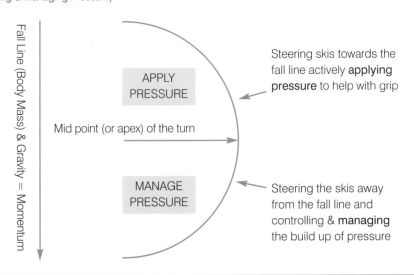

technical

Through the first half of the turn your goal is to get your skis to grip. This can be done by balancing more against the outer ski of your turn either by bracing your leg or by actively stretching your leg and pressing the ski back into the snow thus creating more pressure.

In the second half of the turn you need to manage pressure that is already there due to turning your skis away from the fall line. To clarify; A skier has momentum from sliding down the hill and turning your skis across this line of momentum creates a build up of pressure that must be managed. This is done by allowing your legs to bend and absorb that pressure, which helps with maintaining good balance.

There are a couple of good analogies which help with understanding how pressure control works; When in the gym using the leg press machine you extend or stretch your legs in order to lift the weight (actively applying pressure) while you bend your legs in order to lower the weight (manage the pressure).

Secondly, when you do a press up, you extend your arms to lift your body (apply pressure against the floor) and you bend your arms to lower your weight (manage the pressure).

One final important point with pressure control relates to the speed at which you make these stretching and bending movements of your legs. In other words, you need to distribute your movements to match the size and shape of your turn. If the timing of these movements is not matched to the size of the turn then you may lose grip or contact with the snow, which is fine if you want to un-weight your skis to bring them around more quickly as may be the case on a steep narrow slope.

Edging your skis involves tilting them at an angle so that the edges cut into the snow and help with grip. Assuming that you maintain balance and consequently effective pressure control then, the more you tilt your skis onto their edges, the tighter your turn will be.

One of the most common phrases that I hear skiers say is, "I need to get more edge" when in reality what they need is to maintain effective balance against their outer ski so that the edge can grip. Edging movements can come from the lower leg (knees & ankles), from the hips or the whole body. At higher speeds the body comes further to the inside of the turn.

The mistake that many recreational skiers make is that they edge their skis by moving their whole body inwards at lower speeds and consequently lose balance and grip.

You should aim to edge both skis equally as this promotes good balance and distribution of pressure between your skis.

technical

Equal edge tilt promotes good balance & distribution of pressure

Rotary movements come from turning your legs within the hip socket. This results in pivoting the feet and skis. While both legs work independently of each other the goal is to get the inner leg and ski to copy the outer leg and ski so that there is simultaneous rotation (parallel skiing).

The easiest way to understand and become aware of leg rotation is to do a direct side slip, then pivot your feet & skis 180° so that you can side slip directly down the fall line with the skis facing the other direction. This should be done while keeping the upper body quiet and uninvolved.

Linking direct side slips together is often referred to as **pivot slips** (or pivoting on the line) and is a skill practised by good skiers, leaders and instructors to help focus on the rotary element of steering.

If you can develop your ability and heighten your awareness of each of the steering elements, then you will be in a much better position, to **blend** these elements together to suit the terrain, your speed and the corridor that you wish to ski. Skilful skiers have the ability to use all these elements in order to accurately steer their skis on whatever terrain the mountain throws at them.

2) Progression from Beginner to Parallel

Now that you have read and understood the section on Skiing Fundamentals it is time to look at the stages that learners progress through on the road to becoming "parallel skiers". This section is written so as to give advice to the alpine ski leader. However it is just as useful for the novice skier to read to help them understand their development on the road, or should I say piste, to parallel. Indeed as a keen recreational skier this section will help you to gain a clearer understanding of how skiing works at slower speeds. We can all benefit from occasionally going back to basics. One of my favourite sayings is that "speed masks accuracy"! An important point for ski leaders to take on board here is that your job when leading your groups is to help your students to learn and use the skiing fundamentals so that they continually develop their performance by learning to turn left and right more and more efficiently.

The progression from beginner to parallel simply provides you with a structure so that you can recognise where your learners are on the road to parallel skiing. You need understand how the skiing fundamentals relate to these stages of development so that the movements that your learners make are efficient and effective. Your own performance demonstrating these stages is also crucial so that you create the right picture. What follows is a simple diagram of the stages of development from beginner to parallel:

Diagram 3
(Beginner to Parallel)

STRAIGHT RUNNING
Sliding & balancing

PLOUGHING
Gliding & changing the size of the plough

PLOUGH TURNING
Using turn shape to control speed

PLOUGH PARALLEL
Pivot not push

BASIC PARALLEL
Turning both feet at the same time

PARALLEL USING POLES
Pole touch & pole plant

technical

2.1 Straight Running - sliding and balancing

The goal here is to develop confidence and balance while sliding. Ski Leader's must choose terrain carefully (ideally with a run out) as the control of speed at this point is determined by the terrain. Skiers should be encouraged to balance equally on both skis with the skis flat. A variety of drills can be practiced here to test balance but remember that the goal is to instil confidence. While it is inevitable that skiers will fall over while learning to ski, if beginners are continually falling over then the tasks or the terrain are too difficult. Ski Leaders must take responsibility for ensuring that this does not happen.

2.2 Ploughing - gliding and changing the size of the plough

This is where the skier learns to control speed. However choice of terrain is once again crucial at this stage. If the gradient is too steep then the skier will need to make a large plough shape which will result in poor posture and a defensive approach to skiing.

Remember that "Practice makes permanent", while "Correct practice makes perfect".

The movements required to go from a straight run to a plough are turning of both legs/feet, while displacing the feet slightly wider than the hips. This draws the tips of the skis closer while moving the tails of the skis wider. You need to encourage "rotation" under the foot rather than pushing the tails out! Again a variety of tasks can be practiced here but the goal is to develop a stable gliding plough position on easy terrain. Time spent achieving this is time well spent as turning will be much easier.

2.3 Plough Turning - Using turn shape to control speed

A good stance has now been created over the skis to help maintain balance while sliding over the slippery surface and now it is time to learn how to make turns so that the skier can move down a slope keeping control of both direction and the rate of descent.

It is important to maintain the width of the plough (feet slightly wider than the hips) as the skis start to change direction. Imagine the plough as an arrowhead pointing in the direction the skier wishes to travel. Starting in a gliding plough, directly down the fall line to give slight motion, gently rotate both skis (arrowhead) to the left. On a slight slope the skis will take the skier to the left, keeping a little momentum. Before the skis come to a stop rotate the feet back to centre (fall line) and then to go to the right continue to rotate the feet in that direction. This is the first principle of linking turns.

Once the skis can be changed confidently in both directions it is time to move to a slightly steeper slope to practice the same task but allowing the outside ski to create a natural edge against the snow.

To develop plough turns so that the skier can explore more of the beginners' area safely your learners need to add in some movement from their ankles, knees & hip joints to help the accuracy of the plough turns.

Plough turn sequence from initiation through to completion

When steering the plough towards the fall line the hips should be progressively **stretched** away from the feet by making the legs long (keeping hips above the feet at all times). As rotation happens through the turn, progressively shorten the legs (bending) to a point where there is a feeling of being balanced well against the outside ski, with the skis having been turned sufficiently around the arc. At this point the stretch starts to initiate the next change of direction (back to centre). These movements need to be timed accurately to match the turn shape that the skier is trying to achieve (C shape), thus continuous stretching and bending movement with the legs and rotation of the legs/feet. The complex aspect here is the ability to blend more than one movement together at the same time e.g. stretch & rotate, bend & rotate.

An important fundamental point is, that as the plough turner develops their skill at turning, the overall size of the plough will reduce, with the shape of the turn (curve length) being a crucial element in the control of speed. However for any given set of turns the plough will always remain the same size thus encouraging the turning of **both** feet and avoiding any lateral pushing movements.

2.4 Plough Parallel - pivot not push

Now that the skier has learned to steer the skis accurately in both directions and can keep control of the descent down the hill by the line that is taken, they can be taken a step closer to becoming a parallel skier (which is what every beginner skier strives to be able to achieve - ski leaders should not forget that!).

Moving onto the next level of slope (blue/easy red) will give the skier more momentum and the skis will travel more easily around the arc. With good balance and management of pressure in the second half of the turn, the inside leg/foot can be rotated more than previously. Initially the tips of the skis keep pointing towards each other until safely passed the fall line. At this point separate the inner tip from the outer tip (tips apart) to let the skis become parallel, finishing the arc with a controlled parallel skid.

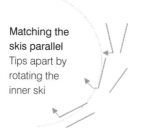

Matching the
skis parallel
Tips apart by
rotating the
inner ski

Diagram 4
(matching your skis parallel)

As long as the terrain does not become steeper or more variable (bumps/chopped up soft snow/slush) the skier will become competent quite quickly at **plough parallel**. The snow and gradient of the slope will help the inside ski to rotate earlier & earlier in the turn. With practice the skier will soon be matching the skis parallel from the fall line.

It is important that the skier is kept in their comfort zone and on familiar terrain so that this development can take place. If the skier is stressed by any of the above they will initially resist matching the skis and increase the size of their plough shape to "keep the brakes on!"

The choice of the word "matching" is very important as the goal is to allow the inside ski to copy the outside one so that both skis are steered in a curve. The distance between the feet in a good plough turn and a plough parallel should not be significantly different. The mistake that many skiers make at this stage is to focus too much on bringing the inner ski parallel, often by sliding it in closer or lifting it in followed by a traverse! The result of this is poor turn shape which creates a block in the skiers' ability to steer both skis parallel.

As skiers and teachers it is better if you can focus on developing the correct movement patterns rather than trying to improve a specific manoeuvre such as plough parallel.

We have looked quite closely at how the skis are matched and steered parallel but it is equally important that the initiation of the turn is such that it is helping the skier to develop towards parallel. Therefore to start the next turn the legs are stretched as before, while the outer foot/ski is pivoted to make a small plough, bringing the outer tip closer to the inner tip (tips together).

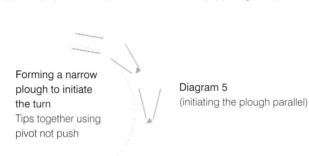

Forming a narrow plough to initiate the turn
Tips together using pivot not push

Diagram 5
(initiating the plough parallel)

Again it is crucially important that the plough size remains small so that the skier's hips flow into the turn. Pushing the foot out would cause breaking and create a blockage in the development towards parallel.

Remember PNP - Pivot not Push!

So we can to an extent simplify the movements in plough parallel as "tips together, tips apart". As the skier improves the duration of the plough will reduce NOT the size of the plough.

2.5 Basic Parallel - turning both feet at the same time

With plough parallel most skiers can travel safely around 80% of the pisted mountain. To get them through that next 20% requires patience from both ski leader and pupil alike.

All the previously learned skills need to be practiced with revision on balance, steering and controlled skidding. The key factors that contribute to "parallel" throughout the turn are increased speed around the curve and an increase in the gradient (but not necessarily both at the same time!) This allows the skier to become effectively balanced against the outer ski earlier and earlier thus making it easier for the inner ski to copy.

This is also the time that the "crossover" effect is felt and becomes more evident. This is where the hips come forward and across the feet as the edges of the skis are changed. In reality this movement is developed in plough parallel provided the movement pattern is correct (as described earlier).

technical

The definition of a parallel turn is when the distance between the tips and the tails remains the same for the whole turn. Both legs/feet are rotated simultaneously and eventually both edges are changed at the same time with the feet about hip width apart. If not challenged by terrain the average skier will naturally progress into parallel turns but if the gradient of the slope is too steep control will be lost very quickly!

2.6 Parallel using Poles - pole touch & pole plant
To help with timing of the turns and the coordinating of all the movements a pole plant can be introduced. Initially lightly touching the snow on the inside of the turn as the stretch is carried out (change of edges) and giving the skier commitment to making the turn. The **pole touch** should be by a movement of the wrist (hands already forwards from the waist) and not a whole upper body swing.

When the skier is ready to move onto steeper slopes and use shorter radius turns the **pole plant** becomes more important. It signals the initiation of the turn and gives an extra point of balance. The pole also gives feedback from the snow - hard packed/soft/powder/hollow/not there at all! This feedback gives additional information that will help you make any adjustments required to complete the turn successfully and in control.

3) Skiing Activities
This section provides Alpine Ski Leaders with some examples of "activities" that they can use with members' of their groups during practice sessions and for their own personal performance development. Each activity is described using a "skills activity card" and these cards are colour coded as follows;

3.1	Light Green	Introductory Activities, Straight Running & Ploughing
3.2	Dark Green	Plough Turning
3.3	Light Blue	Plough Parallel
3.4	Dark Blue	Basic Parallel
3.5	Red	Parallel
3.6	Black	Beyond Parallel

It should be noted that the "colour" is a guide to the most difficult type of terrain that a skier of this level would be able to comfortably ski. However the terrain choice for the activity may be different (quite often easier) depending on the activity itself and the skiing fundamentals being developed.

Here is a list of the activities covered in the ASL Activity Cards;

a) Head, shoulders, knees & boots (Light Green)
b) Copy the actions of the leader (Light Green)
c) Big toe down, big toe up (Dark Green)
d) Follow the leader (Dark Green)
e) Direct side-slip (Light Blue)
f) Tips together, tips apart (Light Blue)
g) Swing to the hill (Dark Blue)
h) Tapping the inside ski/Rock stars (Dark Blue)
i) Carved traverse (Red)
j) 10 toes, 2 toes (Red)
k) Balancing on outside ski (Black)
l) Syncro short radius (Black)

technical

3.1 Light Green - Introductory Activities, Straight Running & Ploughing

ASL Skills Activity Card	
Activity	Head, shoulders, knees & boots
Objective	To develop balance & co-ordination while sliding
Skier Ability	Straight running
Terrain choice	Easy green ideally with a run out
Equipment required	Normal ski equipment (without ski sticks)
Description of Activity	Performance Quality
Both hands touch head, then shoulders then the knees followed by the top of the ski boots while sliding down a gentle slope.	Movements should be made smoothly so as to promote good balance on both skis
Example	

The picture here shows a good straight running position with the skis flat and about hip width apart. Joints lightly flexed, hands in front and away from the body. From here the skier can easily do the activity described above.

ASL Skills Activity Card	
Activity	Copy the actions of the leader
Objective	To test if the skill is in the acquired learner phase
Skier Ability	Ploughing
Terrain choice	Easy green slope
Equipment required	Normal ski equipment (without ski sticks)
Description of Activity	Performance Quality
Leader stands at the bottom of a small slope. Student plough glides directly towards the leader. The leader makes a series of hand actions which the student copies while maintaining a constant rate of descent in the plough	All actions should promote balance on both skis e.g. work in the vertical plane with actions such as hands on hips, hands on knees, arms folded, clapping hands etc.

technical

3.2 Dark Green – Plough Turning

ASL Skills Activity Card	
Activity	Big toe down, big toe up
Objective	To develop a narrow plough (wedge) with the outside ski edged and the inner ski fairly flat
Skier Ability	Plough Turning
Terrain choice	Green slope
Equipment required	Normal ski equipment
Description of Activity	Performance Quality
Skier presses the big toe on the outer ski down, to encourage edge & pressure and then lifts the big toe on the inner ski up, to encourage the ski to flatten.	This is a subtle pressure/edge control activity and its important that the inner ski is flattened but not lifted. This is great preparation for plough parallel.
Example	

In this picture the outer ski (skier's right ski) is beginning to be edged (big toe down) while the inner ski (skier's left ski) is slightly flatter (big toe up)

ASL Skills Activity Card	
Activity	Follow the leader
Objective	To accurately follow the line of the leader and therefore benefit from the rounded shaped turns
Skier Ability	Plough Turning
Terrain choice	Green slope
Equipment required	Normal ski equipment
Description of Activity	Performance Quality
Classic follow the leader activity where the student follows the line (turn shape) of the leader as accurately as possible.	It is essential that the students do not cut the corners as this will not promote good rounded turns. Also if this task is being done with several people in a "snake" then the order must be changed regularly so that everyone benefits from being behind the leader. An alternative here is to pair up the group with stronger and weaker skiers together so that the weaker ones can benefit from the turn shape of the better skiers.

3.3 Light Blue – Plough Parallel

ASL Skills Activity Card	
Activity	Direct side-slip
Objective	To develop good skidding & balance
Skier Ability	Plough Parallel
Terrain choice	Short steep section on red or blue piste
Equipment required	Normal ski equipment
Description of Activity	Performance Quality
From a static position with skis across the fall line release edges and make a continuous sideways slide.	The skis speed should be continuous without deviation from the fall line.
Example	

In this picture the skis are across the fall line and being allowed to slide sideways. It takes practice to allow this speed to be constant and to deal with any build up of snow.

ASL Skills Activity Card	
Activity	Tips together, tips apart
Objective	To develop good leg foot rotational skills
Skier Ability	Plough Parallel
Terrain choice	Blue piste
Equipment required	Normal ski equipment
Description of Activity	Performance Quality
As the skier makes plough parallel turns the focus is on the tips rather than the tails of the skis. This means that as the turn is initiated the outer tip moves towards the inner tip. And as the turn is completed the inner tip moves away from the outer tip.	To ensure that the tips come together and then apart the skier must pivot under the foot. With practice the time delay between tips together and tips apart will reduce until eventually the skier is turning parallel.

3.4 Dark Blue – Basic Parallel

ASL Skills Activity Card	
Activity	Swing to the hill
Objective	To work on completing the turn steering both skis parallel from start to finish with good management of pressure
Skier Ability	Basic Parallel
Terrain choice	Blue piste
Equipment required	Normal ski equipment
Description of Activity	Performance Quality
From either a steep traverse or from the fall line steer the skis in a continuous arc until they face slightly back up the hill and come to a complete stop	Start from a tall position and flex the ankles, knees and hips in unison as the skis are steered around the curve. This is great for developing a smooth blend of the three steering elements.
Example	

In this picture the legs are flexing as the skis are being steered in a continuous arc.

ASL Skills Activity Card	
Activity	Tapping the inside ski/Rock stars
Objective	To develop good balance on the outer ski
Skier Ability	Basic Parallel
Terrain choice	Easy blue terrain
Equipment required	Normal ski equipment
Description of Activity	Performance Quality
Balance against the outside ski while tapping the inside ski on the snow. Initially this can be done in a traverse i.e., balance on the downhill ski and tap the uphill ski. Then start to tap the ski through the end of the curve. With sufficient speed it will be possible to become supported against the outer ski earlier in the turn and tap the inner ski all the way around the curve	The whole ski should be lifted (equal at tip and tail) so as to promote a centrally balanced position. To liven up this activity pretend you are a "rock star" strumming your guitar. Hold your ski sticks as if they were a guitar and as you play your guitar you should stamp your inner ski while turning.

3.5 Red – Parallel

ASL Skills Activity Card	
Activity	Carved Traverse
Objective	To develop edge & pressure control
Skier Ability	Parallel
Terrain choice	Green or blue terrain
Equipment required	Piste skis with good sidecut
Description of Activity	**Performance Quality**
From a steep traverse allow both skis to carve back up the hill until the skis come to a complete stop.	The skis should be tilted (edged) the same amount. Shins should be parallel. The tracks left in the snow should be like tram lines with both skis carving.
Example	

In this picture you can see that both skis are tilted to the same angle with daylight between the legs. This more open stance makes edging easier.

ASL Skills Activity Card	
Activity	10 toes, 2 toes
Objective	Pressure control from fore to middle of the ski
Skier Ability	Parallel
Terrain choice	Blue or red terrain
Equipment required	Piste skis
Description of Activity	Performance Quality
The skier focuses on all ten toes at the initiation of the turn by bringing the hips forward and across so the the front of the skis begin to grip. Then as the turn progresses the focus changes to the big toe on the outside ski and the little toe on the inside ski (2 toes) allowing the pressure to be more central with good edge grip.	The movements of extending the legs and bringing the hips forward and flexing the legs and settling need to be done smoothly. For best results do the activity in long radius turns to begin with so there is time to make gradual movements.

technical

3.6 Black – Beyond Parallel

ASL Skills Activity Card	
Activity	Balancing on outside ski
Objective	To develop balance (fore/aft & lateral)
Skier Ability	Beyond Parallel
Terrain choice	Easy blue progressing to steeper blue
Equipment required	Piste skis with good sidecut
Description of Activity	Performance Quality
Balance on the outside ski and carve complete "C" shaped turns	Transition between turns should be smooth (ideally before the fall line) with the outer ski carving cleanly and maintaining balance on outer ski throughout. The lifted ski should remain parallel and evenly balanced
Example	

IIn this picture you can see that the inside ski has been lifted before the fall line and is evenly balanced.

ASL Skills Activity Card	
Activity	Syncro short radius
Objective	To ski shout radius turns in perfect timing with a partner
Skier Ability	Beyond Parallel
Terrain choice	Steep blue or easy red with continuous pitch
Equipment required	Piste skis
Description of Activity	Performance Quality
Short radius turns shadowing your partner so that you turn at the same time as each other.	Pole plants should be at the same time as each other. And the partner who is "shadowing" should be directly above the skier who is setting the rhythm.
Example	

In this picture you can see that both skiers are in perfect timing with each other..

technical

The activities in this manual are just a few examples of the sorts of things you can do with your students and as ski leaders you should build up your own bank of activities using the format that we have used here.

You could even start by adapting some of the activities that have been used here for different levels of skiers; e.g., follow the leader and syncro skiing can work for different levels and activities like side slipping need to be practised by skiers from good plough turning upwards. The key here is to have easier and more difficult side slip activities!

The key ingredients to successful practice are choosing appropriate activities for the student's ability level and being clear about the purpose of such an activity in terms of developing skiing fundamentals. In others words, WHAT, WHERE and WHY;

- WHAT – what activity is appropriate
- WHERE – where should it be done (terrain choice)
- WHY – why are you doing it (purpose & skiing fundamental being developed)?

leadership and leading

By the end of this section all candidates should be able to:

- State one thing to develop to improve as a leader
- Describe one leadership model
- Outline some key steps in organising a trip
- State some top tips for leading on the hill

1 LEADERSHIP MODELS

1.1 WHAT IS A LEADER?

A Leader is someone who exercises a definite and particular role in relation to others
A Role is a set of expected behaviours associated with a position in a group

'Leadership is a set of identifiable behaviours and functions which are used, not only by the leader, but sometimes by other individuals in the group, which is intended to influence the others in order to achieve particular aims or goals.'

It is only when technical skills are used equally in combination with leader skills and relationship skills that effective leadership can happen consistently. To carry out these functions effectively a leader needs to be able to call on a range of both technical and relationship skills. The technical skills are presented in the other parts of this manual. Some of the more important "people skills" are trainable and can be acquired to assist the leader in performing their role. These skills should be developed from conscious skills into ingrained habits (i.e. from awareness phase, through practice phase until they are acquired).

leadership and leading

1.2 LEADERSHIP COMPETENCIES

Both leading and teaching can be viewed along a spectrum, where at one end all responsibility rests with the leader, and at the other end, decision making is devolved to the learner. As the relationship between the leader and group develops it becomes possible, sometimes necessary or desirable, for the leader to use alternative ways of exercising control.

The leader has to decide which particular approach to use. Leadership is an interactive, two-way process involving both the leader and the learner in decision making and responsibility. A leader requires a wide range of competencies to fulfil the role successfully. Leadership competencies are listed on the table below. They were identified by people attending an Alpine Ski Leader course as being the most important ones for a "Role Model" Alpine Ski Leader to possess. The table has been compiled from exercises conducted on actual ASL courses over a period of 15 years.

KNOWLEDGE/SKILLS	BEHAVIOUR/QUALITIES
Organisational skills	Good organiser
Observation skills	Goal setting
Knowledge of Ski Areas	Common sense
Teaching ability	Lesson planning
Teaching/learning styles	Group control/management
Class management	Sympathetic
Skiing ability	Considerate
Ski Technique	Standards/Discipline
Fault analysis/correction	Likes people
Group members	Responsible
Ski Equipment	Adaptable
Map reading/Navigation	Communicator
Teambuilding	Motivator
Foreign Travel	Timekeeper
Linguistic skills	Patient
First Aid	Sense of Humour
Ski Maintenance	Confident
Bindings	Reliable
Leadership	Positive attitude
Mountain hazards	Listener
Safety issues	Calm in crisis
Appropriately dressed/equipped	Approachable
Piste markers/signs	Punctual/time management
FIS Skiers Code of Conduct	Role model

leadership and leading

Background of Group Weather forecast Ski clothing Emergency/accident procedures Local Authority Policies Presentation skills	Open minded Level headed Professional attitude

The tasks undertaken by an Alpine Ski Leader are very varied and whilst some of them will be no more than second nature, others will require a concentrated effort to be able to carry them out to a suitable standard.

In considering the above table,

• How many do you possess at present?

• How many do you require to develop to become a "Role Model" Alpine Ski Leader?

• What are you going to do to develop them?

It will be useful to prepare an action plan so that the areas for development can be addressed in a realistic and thorough way.

1.3 LEADERSHIP MODELS

There are a number of leadership models which have been used in leadership training. They have become more generally known in outdoor activities since the late 1970's. They are helpful and useful as aids to help leaders to think and develop their own ideas about leadership. Three models will be described in this Chapter. They are the "Action Centred Leadership Model", the Tannenbaum and Schmidt in "Hersey Blanchard Situational Leadership Model"

1.3.1 JOHN ADAIR ACTION CENTRED LEADERSHIP MODEL
In terms of fulfilling many of the Leader's responsibilities, using the Action Centred Leadership Model can be very helpful. The Action Centred Leadership model encourages the leader to have a broad approach to the role and not solely focus on one area which can be all too easy to do.

1.3.2 THE MODEL
The three parts of Adair's Action-Centred Leadership model are commonly represented by three overlapping circles, which is a trademark belonging to John Adair. Adair's famous 'three circles' model is one of the most recognizable and iconic symbols within management theory.

leadership and leading

John Adair's Action-Centred Leadership model is represented by Adair's 'three circles' diagram, which illustrates Adair's three core management responsibilities:

• achieving the task
• building/maintaining the team
• developing individuals

John Adair's action-centred leadership task-team-individual model adapts extremely well for the demands of the Alpine Ski Leader. When using it in your own situation think about the aspects of performance necessary for success, and incorporate local relevant factors into the model to create your own interpretation. This will give you a very useful management framework:

1.3.3 CHECKLISTS
The following checklists are designed to help apply the 3 areas of the leader's responsibility.

Your responsibilities as a leader for achieving the task are:
• identify aims and vision for the group, purpose, and direction - define the activity (the task)
• identify resources, people, processes, systems and tools (inc. financial, communication)
• create the plan to achieve the task - deliverable, measurable, timescales, strategy and tactics
• establish responsibilities, objectives, accountabilities and measures, by agreement and delegation
• set standards, quality, time and reporting parameters
• control and maintain activities against parameters
• monitor and maintain overall performance against plan
• report on progress towards the group's aim
• review, re-assess, adjust plan, methods and targets as necessary

leadership and leading

Your responsibilities as a leader for the group are:
- establish, agree and communicate standards of performance and behaviour
- establish style, culture, approach of the group - soft skill elements
- monitor and maintain discipline, ethics, integrity and focus on objectives
- anticipate and resolve group conflict, struggles or disagreements
- assess and change as necessary the balance and composition of the group
- develop team-working, cooperation, morale and team-spirit
- develop the collective maturity and capability of the group - progressively increase group freedom and authority
- encourage the team towards objectives and aims - motivate the group and provide a collective sense of purpose
- identify, develop and agree team- and project-leadership roles within group
- enable, facilitate and ensure effective internal and external group communications
- identify and meet group training needs
- give feedback to the group on overall progress; consult with, and seek feedback and input from the group

Your responsibilities as a leader for each individual are:
- understand the team members as individuals - personality, skills, strengths, needs, aims and fears
- assist and support individuals - plans, problems, challenges, highs and lows
- identify and agree appropriate individual responsibilities and objectives
- give recognition and praise to individuals - acknowledge effort and good work
- where appropriate reward individuals with extra responsibility, advancement and status
- identify, develop and utilise each individual's capabilities and strengths
- train and develop individual team members
- develop individual freedom and authority

leadership and leading

This model can effectively be used following a period of leadership to check where the leader's focus of attention has been. Over a period of time (e.g. a half or whole day session) it would be expected that a leader would have a reasonable spread of their focus between the task, the team and the individual.

All three areas should be regarded as interlinked in that an over-concentration on one will be to the detriment of the other two. For example, a single-minded concentration by the leader on the task is likely to result in a breakdown of communication with the group. Conversely, concentrating too much on individuals within the group could mean that the attainment of the group's goal is put in jeopardy or never achieved.

This model provides one way for the leader to identify and decide which of the three areas most requires immediate attention in a working situation.

1.3.4 OBSERVATION OF THE LEADER

One way of helping the development of awareness of leadership behaviour is to review a session after leading the group. Imagine there are 100 points to be allocated amongst the three overlapping circles. How many points would be allocated to each one?

If the leader focussed largely on one area to the exclusion of the other two areas, most of the points would be allocated there. If there was equal emphasis then the points should be spread more evenly between the three circles. Reviewers should be able to justify their allocation of points by giving clear examples of how the task was achieved, how each individual was developed and how the team was built and maintained. If the leader had decided, or was required, to focus on one particular area and this was also highlighted in the way the group allocated their 100 points then clearly the intention of the leader will have been successful. This method of review can identify mismatches where a leader thinks they are operating in a particular way but this is not actually what is perceived by the group.

During a period of leadership, all three areas would be expected to have received a balance of the leader's attention.

In his book, "Safety, Risk & Adventure in Outdoor Activities" Bob Barton states:
"A simple model such as the three circles of Task, Team and Individual can help the leader to keep a properly broad view. Too many disasters have arisen from a blinkered approach which has a strong focus only on the task and which loses sight of individuals, the team and the effect the environment has on them."

Imagine a situation late in the day when there is tiredness and the leader needs to reach a tow to get back to resort and time is running out. The majority of leaders will focus mainly on the task of getting there in time. They may also be focussing on navigation (another task). That is a good recipe for an incident.

The good leader will achieve the Task, develop the Individual and build and maintain the Team throughout the entire session.

1.3.5 TANNENBAUM AND SCHMIDT MODEL

Tannenbaum & Schmidt is a useful way of looking at ways a Leader can handle power and control on a group. As group develops into a team and moves from one level to the next - the area of freedom increases and the need for the leader's intervention decreases. Following levels are self-explanatory and easy to understand:

1. Tells:

The leader assesses the situation, the group and the resources available, selects a course of action and tells the group what to do. Reasons may or may not be given. "This is how it is going to be and this is how we will do it...."

---

2. Sells:
The Leader chooses a course of action as before but this time gives reasons and explanations to highlight the advantages of the plan and to persuade the group about its rightness. "I want you to do this because...."

3. Tests:
The Leader identifies and outlines the problem or situation giving some of the relevant background information and possible options. Three will be some discussion but it will be confided tom answering objections rather than an open ended debate before going ahead with the intended course of action. "How do you feel about it?"

4. Consults:
The Leader presents a problem and background thinking as before but then asks the group for ideas and comments with the possibility that the intended decision may or may not be modified. The Leader reserves the right to impose his/her own decision. "What do you think - any comments?"

5. Joins:
The Leader presents the problem and perhaps some of the relevant background information and thinking together with some suggestions for possible solutions. The Leader then asks for ideas and help and joins the group. The final decision is likely to be a consensus, a joint one- the result of real sharing and exchange of views. "What should we do?"

6. Delegates:
The Leader either identifies the problem or responds to problems raised by the group or one of its members. The problem is given to the group for them to solve and arrive at a decision. The leader is committed to following their decision and will be available if necessary for consultation. "Will you three sort that out?"

TELLS	SELLS	TESTS	CONSULTS	JOINS	DELEGATES
Leader		Retains		Control	
	Leader		Shares		Control

Leadership is a variety of roles lying between two extremes. The Leader has to decide which particular style is the most appropriate for any situation.

1.3.6 HERSEY BALANCHARD SITUATION LEADERSHIP MODEL

The Hersey Blanchard Model encouragers the leader to let go control as appropriate and devolve responsibility to individuals and the team as their level of maturity in the situation develops.

1.3.7 THE MODEL

For years, when people talked about leadership style, they identified two extremes - an autocratic (directive) leadership style and a democratic (supportive) leadership style. Autocratic leaders used position, power and their authority to get results, while democratic leaders used personal power and involved others in participative problem-solving and decision-making processes.

Hersey and Blanchard in "Leadership and Administration of Outdoor Pursuits" by Phyllis Ford and James Blanchard (1985), tell us that the continuum between human relationships and the accomplishment of tasks, one's leadership style, will depend on two variables: the level of maturity of the group of followers and the demands of the situation.

The demands of the situation relate to the task to be accomplished. In outdoor pursuits the situation may range from formal to informal, tense to relaxed, dangerous to safe. It may demand a great amount of leader control or little or no control.

Situation demands little leader control	Situation needs some leader control	Situation demands complete leader control
Towards the end of a week's session the leader may wait at the bottom of a short easy run where both the top and bottom of the uplift can be seen and the whole of the slope ask the group to do 2 warm up runs.	Using "Practice" style of teaching where the task is determined by the leader (e.g. snowplough turn) but the individuals determine the size of the turn and how many to do,	At the start with a new group. Any time when safety is an issue

leadership and leading

Further research showed that leadership styles tend to vary considerably from situation to situation, and that it is not helpful to think of leadership style as an either/or continuum. While the behaviour of some leaders is characterised mainly by directing their followers' activities in terms of task accomplishment (directive behaviour), other leaders concentrate on providing socio-emotional support and on building personal relationships between themselves and their followers (supportive behaviour). In other situations, various combinations of directive and supportive behaviour are evident. Thus, it was determined that directive and supportive leader behaviours are not either/or leadership styles. Instead, these patterns of leader behaviour can be plotted on two separate and distinct axes.

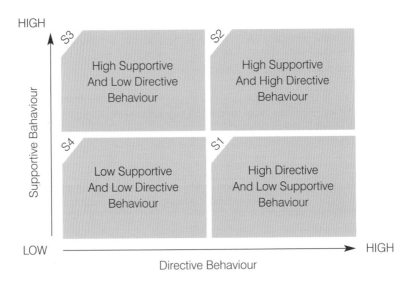

1.3.8 DIRECTIVE AND SUPPORTIVE LEADER BEHAVIOURS

Directive behaviour is defined as:
The extent to which a leader engages in one-way communication, spells out the follower(s) role and tells the follower(s) what to do, where to do it, when to do it and how to do it, and then closely supervises performance. Three words can be used to define directive behaviour: structure, control, supervise.

Supportive behaviour is defined as:
The extent, to which a leader engages in two-way communication, listens, provides support and encouragement, facilitates interaction and involves the follower(s) in decision making.
Three words can be used to define supportive behaviour: praise, listen and facilitate.

In style 1 (S1) a leader is high on direction, low on support. S/he defines roles and goals, provides specific instruction to the follower(s), and closely supervises task accomplishment. When using style 2 (S2) the leader is high on both direction and support. S/he explains decisions and solicits suggestions from the follower(s), but continues to direct task accomplishment. Style 3 (S3) leader behaviour is characterised by high supportive low directive behaviour. The leader and follower(s) make decisions together and then the leader supports the followers' efforts toward task accomplishment. In style 4 (S4), a leader provides low support and direction. S/he turns over decisions and responsibility for implementation to the follower(s)

Styles of Leadership

Each of the four leadership styles outlined on the previous page can be identified with a different approach to problem solving and decision making as described below.

The styles of leadership model explanations are amended and reproduced with the author's permission from "Leading and Managing Groups in the Outdoors", by Ken Ogilvie.

S1- Directing High directive/Low supportive leader behaviour

This style is well illustrated in the early stages of a group's life when the members are uncertain of each other, not too sure about the leader and a bit hazy about the objective. The important thing is to get the task moving by feeding in much information and perhaps imparting a lot of skill. In this situation the leader will be doing a lot of telling and directing and staying in charge. Personal feelings and group needs will be secondary to the achievement of the task. Emergencies would come into this category. The maturity (development stage) of the group is low and the leader may well have a very impersonal relationship with the group.

S2 - Coaching High directive/High supportive leader behaviour

In this situation the leader will be active and visible but not necessarily directive. A lot is going on, such as in the "early" phase of a new group's life. Questions to do with 'why' rather than 'what' are being asked, so reasons and explanations are required in order to persuade and convince e.g. Why do we have to on this run rather than down that one?

---

leadership and leading

Good relationships are as important as getting on with the job because at this juncture if the relationship becomes soured the task may not be achieved. At this stage the leader's role tends to become political and diplomatic in essence, particularly when conflicts, a feature of this phase, have to be resolved positively. In other words, to be effective, the leader has to be flexible in order to be able to adapt to a variety of conditions or situations. The sustained exercise of a single leadership style here might well be disastrous.

S3 - Supporting High Supportive/Low directive leader behaviour
Here, roles have been assigned to, or assumed by, group members with the skills and ability to undertake them. Control of some things is moving naturally away from the leader. But it is important that, with the removal of this cohesive influence, group harmony is maintained so that various parts continue to work together. In order not to become too distant from the group, it is now possible for the leader's focus to move away from the task, and concentrate more on the needs and wants of the group and individuals within it. The leader will thus participate on a level nearer to the group by joining, sharing, testing and consulting. On some expeditions leadership never gets beyond this phase because of a leader's need to feel that his/her group remain dependant. This is a limited view and can be considered as unjust or selfish in that it blocks the development of others.

S4 - Delegating Low supportive/Low directive leader behaviour
In this situation the leader allows his/her role to become low key in order that the group is able to become self functioning to the extent that it, or individuals in it, can see what needs to be done, set up tasks, take most of the decisions and carry them out. The leader will be mostly delegating, consulting a little, supervising a lot and monitoring all the time. A physical example of this sort of situation would be a group well on the way to self sufficiency as say with an established, fairly well trained and experienced group, preparing to go on a ski trip as part of the training for the Duke of Edinburgh Award Scheme. There is a possibility of becoming confused here: within the group there will need to be high supportive behaviour in order to carry out a task that may be simple at times and complex at others. So how does this fit into a category of Low supportive/Low directive behaviour? The distinguishing feature here is that the relationship between leader and the group needs to be less involved.
Relating situational demands to group maturity or development tells us that the leader's style will change depending on the task/relationship orientation as well as group maturity.

To further illustrate the four dimensions above, assume a group of adults is starting their first ski trip. As a whole, the group's knowledge, skills, and ability to take responsibility for it is very limited (immature), and safety is a prime concern of the leader who would use a directive approach with little interaction with the learners. However, leadership style would change to a point where it might even be participative, as the learners develop their skills and maturity in the activity and become as adept as their leader. Some leaders' own behaviour may be 'locked' at the outer edge of the two axes in figure 1. In other words, leaders who 'need' to be 'in charge' at all times may find it uncomfortable to develop a 'supportive behaviour' role. Similarly, some leaders may find it hard to take control and this may not be appropriate in certain situations where safety is an issue.

leadership and leading

There are some psychometric tests which can be used to determine a leader's comfort zone and some people need to make a considerable effort to operate as a well rounded leader who considers and achieves group development, as well as task achievement.

1.3.9 SUMMARY

Implicit in all that has been written about leadership are a number of general functions specifically pertinent to the exercise of leadership. The more important ones are:

- responsibility
- control
- care
- support
- decision making
- sustaining the group's energy
- setting and maintenance of standards and limits
- flexibility
- engagement and commitment of personal energy to the group's achievement of its task
- awareness of and responsiveness to one's own feelings, wants and needs, and those of the group as individuals and as a whole

leadership and leading

2 THE LEADER AS AN ORGANISER

Before, during and following an outing (particularly a residential ski trip) there are many things a leader will be responsible for. They include planning, supervision, travelling, risks and emergencies

2.1 PLANNING

It is good practice, especially when leading school groups, for the Leader to:
- have a sound reason for the trip. It should be beneficial to pupils and have add on value to what can be achieved in school
- have a clear plan of all activities to be undertaken and their educational objectives;
- have prior knowledge of the venue - the group leader should normally have made an exploratory visit.
- prepare a risk assessment for the entire trip
- follow employers procedures for approval of the trip (this will include information to parents, pupil selection, parents evenings etc)
- consult and comply with all relevant LA/school procedures (particularly for First Aid, dealing with Clinical Waste, Administration of Prescribed Medication, Use of Mobile Phones, Child Protection, Bullying, Disability Discrimination etc)
- set up an approved financial system for fee collection and paying invoices in line with the employers financial procedures
- decide where to go and when to go
- engage an appropriate travel company with the appropriate safeguards
- be competent to exercise appropriate control of the group, and to ensure that pupils abide by the agreed standards of behaviour;
- comply with the employer's emergency procedures and be able to carry them out;
- have appropriate access to First Aid;
- establish the means to contact the home based contact/colleagues/other supervisors if needing help;
- have a preparation plan for pupils so they are ready to take full advantage of the experience

leadership and leading

2.2 SUPERVISION

This is the major responsibility which the Leader undertakes. The responsibility is both constant and total. There are no occasions during a trip when a leader may abdicate this responsibility and the position of being in "loco parentis" cannot be delegated. The Leader is also responsible for ensuring that there is, at all times, an adequate level of supervision. It is likely that the Leader in charge of the trip will have demonstrable experience/ skills in recognising/supporting the broader welfare/pastoral needs of participants which may arise during the course of a residential trip.

It is good practice, especially when leading school groups, for the Leader to:
* ensure an adequate level of supervision for the physical and emotional capabilities of the individuals and the demands of the trip and conditions likely to be encountered.
* appoint an appropriate number of supervising adults;
* ensure all accompanying adults have enhanced disclosure checks;
* have a suitable adult: pupil ratio (normally one ASL per group of no more than 10 pupils).
* ensure that each accompanying adult has a pastoral group plus another key function. All staff must know their exact role and be capable of carrying it out.
* confirm everyone instructing an activity is appropriately qualified

Off Snow Activities
Group leaders should ensure that pupils continue to be properly supervised during downtime before, between and after sessions, including the evenings on residential visits. A group occupied in study or activity is far safer than a group left to its own devices in an unfamiliar environment. Too much unstructured free time in a residential programme can allow time for mischief, bullying, homesickness and wandering off from the body of the group.
It is good practice to:
* ensure that all staff and pupils understand the standards of behaviour that apply at all times, not just during activities;
* ensure that handover between sessions is properly supervised (when using a ski school for part of
* the day on the hill), with a named leader responsible for the group.
* ensure that all leaders understand that their supervisory role continues in the evening - however hard a day it has been.
* It is best to organize a full evening of activities for the group. Each leader could be asked to prepare an evening of activities. (examples of these include. Setting up a short Orienteering course around the hotel or if using a small village it could be wider than the hotel area, bingo in or the language of the country. Interviewing local native speakers with a Dictaphone using a prepared script - this can then be used back at school in class). All it requires is some enthusiasm and creative thinking.
* use down time after activities for individual reflection on personal learning outcomes, and group discussion about the highs and lows of the day;

leadership and leading

Night Time

Group leaders should ensure that:

- the group's immediate accommodation is exclusively for the group's use;
- leaders (of both genders where appropriate) have sleeping accommodation on the same floor immediately adjacent to the pupils' accommodation;
- there is a leader present on that floor whenever the pupils are there;
- child protection arrangements are in place to protect both pupils and staff;
- where hotel/hostel reception is not staffed 24 hours a day, security arrangements should be in force to stop unauthorised visits;
- in the absence of 24 hour staffing of reception, external doors must be made secure against intrusion and windows closed as necessary to prevent intrusion;
- where possible, internal doors are lockable but staff must have reasonable access to the pupil accommodation at all times;
- where pupils' doors are locked, leaders have immediate access, as necessary, to a master key;
- all staff and pupils know the emergency procedures/escape routes in the event of a fire. Where windows and doors are locked against intrusion at night, ensure that alternative escape routes are
- known and that all fire doors function properly.

Don't be lulled into a sense of false security by local assurances, such as "no need to lock doors in this part of the country". The presence of the group may attract unwelcome attention that is unusual in the locality.

2.3 TRAVELLING

Whether travelling by coach or plane the most challenging times are where pupils arrive at a decision making place. This could be a choice of which door to enter, whether to go through a door into an open area or something similar. It is best practice to eliminate decision making opportunities by careful group management. A large group of 50 or 60 are best managed in small groups of up to 10 with a leader in charge of each group with close group control when on the move.

If travelling by coach, a driver cannot safely drive and supervise children at the same time. The leaders should ensure that:

- transport by road has seat belts and that the pupils wear them;
- there is adequate supervision at all times when travelling;
- leaders have reserved seats that allow them to supervise properly
- pupils are supervised when boarding and leaving;
- extra care is taken when leaving a vehicle in a country that drives on the right as some doors may open onto the road side;
- standards of behaviour are met, and in particular that drivers are not distracted
- smoking/alcohol etc. bans are observed;

leadership and leading

- pupils are occupied on long journeys - this will help the journey pass quickly;
- evacuation procedures are clearly understood by everyone, luggage is securely stored and emergency exits are kept clear;
- there are adequate rest stops for drivers;
- head counts are carried out when the group is getting off or onto transport and when the bus stops for refueling or any other unscheduled stop.

Each pupil should:
- know who their leader is at any given time and how to contact him or her;
- have been given clear, understandable and appropriate instructions;
- rarely if ever be on their own;
- alert the leader if someone is missing or in difficulties;
- have a meeting place to return to, or an instruction to remain where they are, if separated;
- understand and accept the expected standards of behaviour.

All leaders should:
- have a reasonable prior knowledge of the pupils including any special educational needs, medical needs or disabilities;
- carry a list/register of all group members, preferably with pictures
- directly supervise the pupils particularly important when they are mingling with the public and may not be easily identified;
- regularly check that the entire group is present;

Head Counts
Whatever the length and nature of the visit, regular head counting of pupils should take place, particularly before leaving any venue. It is good practice for all leaders to:
- carry a list/register of all pupils and adults involved in the trip at all times;
- ensure that pupils are readily identifiable, especially if the visit is to a densely populated area.
- avoid identification that could put pupils at risk e.g. name badges (though some schools find it useful to provide pupils with badges displaying the name of the school or hotel and an emergency contact number, or for visits abroad a note in the language of the country being visited);
- ensure that all pupils are aware of rendezvous points;
- ensure that all pupils know what to do if they become separated from the group.

'Buddy' system
Each child is paired with a buddy. Each regularly checks that the other is present and is OK. A variant of this is the 'circle buddy' system - the pupils form a circle at the start of the visit so that each pupil has a left side buddy and a right side buddy. He or she will check on these when asked. Thus two pupils cannot vanish together and not be missed (as might happen with paired buddies).

leadership and leading

2.4 RISKS AND EMERGENCIES

Careful emergency planning can mitigate the trauma of being caught up in an emergency. It is good practice for the group leader to:

• agree an emergency action plan, which includes 24-hour (i.e. constant cover) contact points at the school/LA and clear roles for the group leader, school/LA contact, head teacher e.g. managing media interest, supporting parents of an injured pupil, transport arrangements etc.;
• ensure that all members of the group know what action to take if there is a problem;
• hold evening briefings with assistants/colleagues to discuss issues for the next day;
• spend time early the next morning explaining arrangements to the pupils;
• hold, and ensure that other adults in the group hold, up-to date competence in first aid.
• ensure that the first aid kit is properly stocked and accessible
• ensure that all pupils' medical needs (e.g. asthma, diabetes, anaphylaxis) are known and that the employer's Policy for the Voluntary Administration of Prescribed Medication is followed;
• recognise that many of the health problems of pupils on longer visits are caused by lack of food, of liquid or of sleep;
• advise group members about the dangers of over-exertion in the heat and of dehydration, which can cause headache, dizziness and nausea;
• on hot days, keep fluid levels high, and use suitably factored sun protection creams and hats/glasses;
• ensure that all pupils understand and follow the code of conduct;
• practice emergency drills e.g. evacuation of bus;

Ongoing Risk Assessment

Risk assessment does not end when the visit begins. Changes to the itinerary, changes to the weather, incidents (whether minor or major), staff illness - all or any of these may bring pupils face to face with unexpected hazards or difficulties and give rise to the need to re-assess risk. The group leader (and other adults with responsibility) will carry out ongoing risk assessments while the visit is taking place. These normally consist of judgements and decisions made as the need arises. They are not usually recorded until after the visit. They should be informed by the generic and visit or site specific risk assessments. It is good practice to have briefings each night to take stock and assess the circumstances for the next day, and to spend time early the next morning explaining arrangements to the pupils.

Check the local weather forecast
- to inform decisions on appropriate clothing;
- to be aware of whether skiing at altitude might be subject to dramatic changes of weather; potential for fallen trees, avalanches etc.
- Seek local knowledge of potential hazards, e.g.
- avalanche areas
- difficult terrain and unstable cliffs
- crossing points for road,

Alternative plans
- good forward planning will always include alternative plans in case there is a need to change;
- leaders faced with potential difficulties will feel more confident to change the plan if a pre-assessed alternative is available;
- regardless of whether alternatives have been pre-assessed, always take time to reassess risks if the plan changes;
- on arrival at a site or activity that has not previously been risk assessed, it is recommend that the leader should risk assess the situation before starting;
- a change of location might involve hazards not covered in the original risk assessment.

Behaviour problems, illness or injury
- poor behaviour may be reduced by ensuring that all pupils are signed up to agreed standards of behaviour before the trip;
- residential trips can be a good opportunity for school staff to get to know pupils away from the confines of the school. But the leader should resist any temptation to accept lower standards of behaviour. The different hazards that pupils may be exposed to away from the school will require them to observe standards of behaviour that are at least as high as, or higher than, in school;
- group leaders should trust their own knowledge of the young people and use their own professional judgment;
- this may include challenging a ski school instructor where the leader's knowledge of the group is superior, or intervening to prompt a change of plan.

leadership and leading

Emergency procedures framework during the visit

If an emergency occurs on a trip the leader should maintain or resume control of the group overall. The main factors to consider include:

- establish the nature and extent of the emergency as quickly as possible;
- ensure that all the group are safe and looked after;
- establish the names of any casualties and get immediate medical attention;
- ensure that a teacher/responsible adult member of the group accompanies casualties to hospital with any relevant medical information, and that the rest of the group are adequately supervised at all times and kept together;
- notify the police if necessary;
- ensure that all group members who need to know are aware of the incident;
- ensure that all group members are following the emergency procedures and the roles allocated to them - revise procedures and re-allocate roles as necessary;
- Inform the home based contact/school contact and provider/tour operator (as appropriate). The school contact number should be accessible at all times during the visit;
- details of the incident to pass on to the school should include: nature, date and time of incident; location of incident; names of casualties and details of their injuries; names of others involved so that parents can be reassured; action taken so far; action yet to be taken (and by whom);
- school contact should notify parents, providing as full a factual account of the incident as possible;
- notify insurers, especially if medical assistance is required (this may be done by the school contact);
- ascertain phone numbers for future calls. Try not to rely solely on mobile phones;
- write down accurately and as soon as possible all relevant facts and witness details and preserve any vital evidence;
- keep a written account of all events, times and contacts after the incident;
- complete an accident report form as soon as possible. Contact HSE or local authority inspector, if appropriate;
- no-one in the group should speak to the media. Names of those involved in the incident should not be given to the media as this could cause distress to their families. Refer media enquiries to a designated media contact in the home area;
- no-one in the group should discuss legal liability with other parties, nor sign anything relating to accident liability without clear advice from their LA;
- keep receipts for any expenses incurred - insurers will require these.

leadership and leading

3 LEADING ON THE HILL

This will be one of the key functions of the leader as seen by the group. They will expect to enjoy the day, learn new skills, and not get lost amongst other things. In order to lead effectively on the hill a number of "Top Tips for Leading" have been developed. This list was prepared by clients attending ASL courses and collected over a period of three years (around 24 courses). Following each session on leading groups on the hill, a full review was conducted for each person leading. At the conclusion of that review the person who had just been reviewed was asked what had been learned then to turn these learning points into top tips to give to the next person to lead. These top tips have been collected and sorted into 5 headings for ease of use. They are listed below.

3.1 TOP TIPS FOR LEADING

BEFORE
- PLAN WELL AND THOROUGHLY
- SET RULES AND CONVEY THEM
- HAVE AN APPROPRIATE SAFETY BRIEFING
- DO A KIT CHECK BEFORE DEPARTING FROM
  THE HOTEL AND INCLUDE EVERYONE

DURING
- SELECT AN APPROPRIATE STYLE
- STAY IN ROLE MODEL THROUGHOUT THE DAY
- MONITOR AND CONTROL THE GROUP
- ENFORCE RULES INCLU DING SAFETY
- VARY POSITION IN GROUP, SOMETIMES IN FRONT, SOMETIMES MIXED WITHIN THE GROUP
  AND SOMETIMES AT THE REAR
- DELEGATE RESPONSIBILITIES AS APPROPRIATE

leadership and leading

- MAKE REGULAR HEAD COUNTS
- MAKE THE TRIP FLOW WITHOUT TOO MANY STOPS

COMMUNICATION - This should be
- CLEAR
- CONCISE
- DECISIVE

It should
- GENERATE CONFIDENCE

Remember to
- LISTEN
- GIVE FEEDBACK TO EVERYONE AS NECESSARY

ACTIVITIES - They should be
- SUFFICIENT
- APPROPRIATE
- ENJOYABLE

LEADER BEHAVIOUR - He/she should be:
- CONFIDENT
- FLEXIBLE
- FAIR
- HONEST
- ENTHUSIASTIC
- ENCOURAGING
- CALM IN CRISIS

And effectively use
- USE OF HUMOUR
- SANCTIONS &/OR REWARDS

The more of these top tips a leader can embrace the more likely the session will be successful.

3.2 SKIWAY CODE

The following rules have been formulated for all practitioners of this sport for the same reason as the Highway Code. If we all do it the same way, we will all know what to expect in given situations, and we will all be safer. The code has been known under a number of themes over the years, such as It is important that these safety rules are conveyed to everyone in the group and applied.

leadership and leading

"Be Aware, Ski with Care", "Don't Be a Toad, Use the Skiway Code", and more recently the SNSC leaflet stated "Get a Grip on Slope Safety, Follow The Snow Code". All of these safety campaigns originated in the FIS safety rules which originated in the 1980's and were reworded and agreed in 2002.

1 Respect for others.
All slope users must behave in such a way that they do not endanger others nor harm them by their behaviour or their equipment.

2 Control of speed and behaviour.
All slope users must adapt their speed and behaviour to their personal capabilities as well as to the general conditions of the slope, weather, snow conditions, and density of other slope users at the time.

3 Choice of the direction by the slope user above.
The slope users who are higher up the slope are in a position which enables them to choose their trajectory. They must always make this choice in a way that they do not endanger the slope users below.

4 Overtaking.
Overtaking may take place above or below, but must always be effected with sufficient space to take into account the movement of the slope user being overtaken.

5 Entering, starting off from and crossing slopes.
When entering and starting off from or crossing slopes, all slope users must visually check uphill and down to ensure that they can do so without endangering themselves or other slope users.

6 Stopping.
All slope users must avoid stopping in narrow places or areas of restricted visibility. In the event of a fall, they should remove themselves from the slope as quickly as possible.

7 Walking up or downhill.
Any slope user who is obliged to move up or downhill on foot must keep to the side of the slope and ensure that neither he nor his equipment endangers other slope users.

8 Respect for information, signs and sign-posting.
All slope users must respect slope information, concerning weather conditions, the conditions of the slopes, and of the snow. They must respect signs and sign posting at all times.

9 Assistance.
Any person who is a witness or instigator of an accident must give assistance, in particular by raising the alarm. Should the need arise, and at the request of the mountain rescue service, he must place himself at their disposal.

10 Identification.
Any person who is involved in, or witness to, an accident must identify themselves to the Ski Patrol, as well as to any others involved in the accident

leadership and leading

3.3 HOW TO LEAD

This is one of the most frequent decisions a Leader will have to make. This decision will be based on judgement. The definition of Judgement is:
"The term judgement generally refers to the considered evaluation of evidence in the formation of making a decision."

Good judgement requires careful and sometimes swift consideration of all of relevant factors some of which may be assumptions. Some people seem to always make good decisions whilst others never seem to get it right. One of the most significant aspects of making a good call is the use of experience. Good Leaders frequently call on past experiences when attempting to reach a decision. The decision on how to lead a group will be determined by careful reflection about the experience of the group, the level of maturity of the group on the hill, the Leaders preferred style of leadership, the group's ability to accept some responsibility for themselves, the weather and snow conditions on the day, the level of fitness of the individual group members on the day, etc. The Leader is constantly making judgements and only experience will ensure that good judgements are made with consistency.

In terms of actual leading on the hill from one place to another sometimes the Leader needs to be in front to navigate accurately whilst at other times, if the person allocated the job of being in front can be trusted to stop at the agreed point, the Leader may be within the group encouraging some and reinforcing some point of technique to others. If getting a group member to lead it is often best to point out some stopping place. e.g. "Do you see the second pylon to the left side of the piste? Stop there with the whole group"

Better still if the piste is already well known to the group then an already known landmark can be used. Under these circumstances it is better to ensure that as Leader you can have all or most of the group in view all or most of the time. Keeping the group compact will prevent difficulties, especially if someone has a problem and there is the risk of the group fragmenting.

Never let the group become so spread out that even some are out of sight for any length of time. If at the front this will mean having regular looks back and if at the rear being able to manage the speed of the group effectively. There are no hard and fast rules about where the leader should be positioned in the group. This will require leader judgement. However if navigation is a problem,(e.g. poor visibility) the leader will be in front, leading slowly, stopping regularly and frequently and making regular head counts. Common sense has to be applied at all times in determining where a leader is within the group.

4 SUMMARY

Irrespective of the leadership model selected or leadership style used a competent leader will have the following said about him/her.

Will it be said about you?
- Is human and treats team members as human beings
- Has no favourites and doesn't bear grudges
- Is easy to talk to and you can tell s/he listens
- Keeps his/her word and is honest
- Doesn't dodge unpleasant issues
- Explains why or why not
- Is fair with praises and criticisms and criticises without making enemies
- Is fair to everyone
- Drives himself so hard you don't mind him expecting the best of you

By the end of this section all candidates should be able to:

- Describe how to navigate in a ski area
- State how to get and use weather forecasts
- Describe a snowpack
- State what to do if you witness an avalanche
- Describe what to do in the event of an accident
- State how to treat and avoid hypothermia
- Describe how to carry out a risk assessment

1 Navigation

1.1 Using a Piste Map

One of the key functions of a Ski Leader is to be able to navigate around a resort safely and without getting lost. Piste maps are artist's impressions of the area and it is sometimes difficult to read a piste map accurately.

Look at the piste map below. Around the Zerotta area it is difficult to work out which direction some of the pistes run. A contour map of the same area gives a clear picture of which way the slopes are facing. It is not usual to buy a local contour map but it has its uses. Look at the one below which is for the same area as the Piste map below and you will note how more detailed and accurate information is available from it.

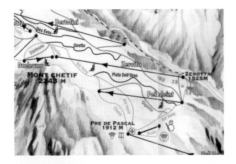
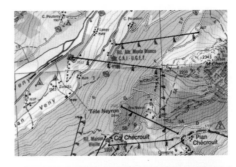

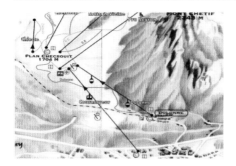 

Maps can get out of date quite quickly. This is an example of a piste map being more up to date than the contour map. The piste map shows a new uplift (Dolonne) whilst the contour map does not include it. Check dates on maps to get an indication of their level of accuracy. Generally a new piste map is likely to be produced if a new uplift is installed whereas a contour map may not be updated for several years.

All maps use symbols and what they represent are stated on the map itself. A Piste map contains lots of useful information as well as showing the lifts and pistes.

1.2 Setting a Map

Setting or orientating a map is the technique of positioning the map so that all the features are lined up with your own location as the central point. What is in front of you on the ground will be in front of you on the map, what is to your left on the ground will also be to your left on the map and so on. The writing on the map may be upside down or sideways but this is OK - having the map set is far more useful in relating the map to the ground than being able to read the writing. View the map as a three-dimensional model which you have lined up with the features on the ground.

In good visibility you may be able to set the map by eye. Once you are on the hill you will need to identify prominent features on the ground such as hills, ridges, valleys and uplifts (maybe there's a village within view) and turn the map so that the features on the ground line up with you at the centre. Both of the maps on the next page are set. The piste map has been drawn looking south so the contour map has to be orientated 180° to match it.

If identifiable features are not visible you can set the map by using the compass. Use the magnetic needle to find north and line up north on the map with north on the ground. There is no need to make any adjustments or bearings with your compass - you are just using the magnetic needle to find north. The side edges of the map will also be pointing north.

 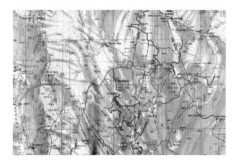

Keep the map set when you change direction. As you turn to face another direction you must also turn the map to keep it correctly set. If your body turns to the right, your hands must turn the map to the left. Whilst this technique is very accurate when using a contour map because of the impressionist nature of a Piste map only a rough setting can be achieved. However this will be sufficient to identify pistes and lifts which will aid navigation.

If new to an area, as well as seeking local knowledge, it is useful to look at one of the large maps often found at the top or bottom of major uplifts or near a gondola station. This will enable the Leader to get a "feel" for the layout of the entire area as well as giving information on avalanche safety, current air temperature and which lifts are open.

1.3 Piste Classification

Pistes are:

- Groomed (dependent on snow conditions)
- Patrolled

Europe:		
	Green	Easy
	Blue	Moderate
	Red	Intermediate
	Black	Difficult

North America:		
	Green	Easiest
	Blue	More difficult
	Black ◆	Most difficult
	Black ◆ ◆	Expert

Australian and New Zealand:		
	Green	Beginner
	Blue	Intermediate
	Black	Advanced
	Black ◆ ◆	Expert Only

Be aware that piste classifications vary in different ski resorts and countries - for example, a blue run in Val d'Isere, France, may be classed a red run if it were in Seefeld, Austria. Often an entire run might be of Blue standard but one steeper pitch might result in it being classified as Red.

Piste conditions change hourly, and what was a cruising blue run mid morning, could be treacherous, difficult, and more like a hard red by 4.00pm. Note that this also works in reverse, and sometimes a quiet red at the end of the day may be a lot easier than an icy and crowded blue.

Note: there can be local and national variations in signs, rules and regulations. When you arrive in a resort, you should obtain and study the piste/trail map of the area.

Off piste areas are:
• Not groomed
• Not patrolled
• For experienced skiers only
• Normally marked by a yellow or Day-Glo orange sign (dashed line on piste map)
• Not for Alpine Ski Leaders with groups

1.4 Navigating around the ski area

Once the Leader has a degree of map literacy and has set the map then pistes and lifts should be easy to identify. Lifts and pistes are usually named and there can be signs usually at the top of lifts and at junctions which further aid navigation.

Don't hesitate to check where you are by using all of the information available including the colour coding of runs. Begin to think ahead and note if you should be passing below a chairlift or if you should be on a piste adjacent to a Poma. All of these clearly identifiable features should be used to confirm accuracy when navigating.

1.5 Navigating in difficult conditions

If you've ever skied in low visibility weather and experienced a "white out," you know how disorienting skiing in fog can be. Beginner runs seem like they could be black. Unseen obstacles - whether they are bumps, snow fences or even other skiers - can not only confuse you, but they are also safety hazards that can cause a collision. Skiing in low visibility is challenging, but if you are careful, you can still ski safely. Here are tips on safe skiing in foggy conditions.

- **Wear goggles**. While wearing goggles won't "clear" the fog completely, a pair of goggles will certainly help you. Goggles with amber lenses that are yellow, orange, or brown tinted will allow you to see a little more definition in the snow.
- **Keep your speed under control.** In low visibility conditions, some obstacles can't be easily spotted and thus are hard to avoid. If you're speeding, it may be too late to swerve around a bump or even avoid another skier. Keeping your speed under control will be safer for everyone on the slope.
- **Watch other skiers in front of you**. While still keeping your eyes on the piste, don't be afraid to take note of others skiers. Remember to keep a safe distance, but watch how the skiers in front of you deal with the terrain - are they slowing down, swerving around a few bumps, or skidding on ice? By watching the skiers in front of you, you can prepare yourself for the terrain that is yet to come.
- **Stick close together.** Make sure you stay close together. With low visibility, it's very easy to miss a turn or take the wrong trail. Make a plan to meet at a central place and carry cell phones or walkie-talkies in case you get separated.
- **Use your poles**. Using your poles to make turns is essential for keeping your balance (and balance is key in foggy weather), but also provides you with an insight to the feel of the snow.
- **Ski only on pistes that you feel confident skiing on**. Dense fog can make a novice trail seem a lot more difficult than it really is. If you're unsure about a trail in clear weather, taking on a trail that may exceed your abilities is simply dangerous in foggy conditions.

When leading a group, as well as keeping safe it is important to navigate well and not lose anyone. This can be achieved by the following strategies.
- Identify which piste you are on by the piste markers so that you know which route to follow down.
- Identify which side of the piste you are at so that you remain on piste. In some countries the markers at the edge of the piste have the tops painted a bright colour. The markers at the right side have a longer bright marking than those on the left.
- In France the piste markers on your right are marked at the top with luminous orange so that you know if you stay to the left of them you are on piste. This is very useful for flat light and whiteout conditions
- Listen for a lift which can be followed down.
- Try to identify pylons adjacent to the piste which can be followed down
- Use a buddy system
- Have a sensible back marker preferably with high viz clothing.
- Stop at frequent intervals after short distances and keep counting your group
- Reassure everyone and stay in a positive confident mode

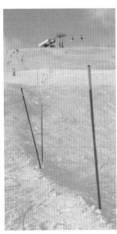

mountain awareness

2 Weather

2.1 Weather Forecasts

These are now readily available from a range of sources.

In Scotland the Mountain Weather Information Service (MWIS) MWIS currently produce forecasts for 8 different mountain areas of the UK as an aid to mountain safety. These forecasts are now viewed by 2 million visitors to the website a year, and can be read on the appropriate webpage, downloaded as a printable PDF, or accessed via internet enabled mobile phone. The production of the Scottish forecasts is fully funded by the Scottish Government through Sportscotland with the support of The Mountaineering Council of Scotland.

To find out a weather report for a ski area is a simple task online. Most of the forecasts give an indication of wind direction and speed as well as precipitation. This information is very out useful for the Leader to be able to brief their group about likelihood of cold condition, wind chill and the possibility of frostnip for example. This could lead to advice about an extra layer being worn or carried and face protection being used. All weather conditions will provide information on temperature, precipitation, wind and cloud.

Temperature

Air is compressible, so when it is stirred the up-currents expand and cool (like air expanding from a tyre valve), whereas down-currents contract and warm (like air compressed in a tyre pump). When air has been well stirred some time during the previous few days, as is often the case, its temperature decreases upwards - on average by about 6°C in every 1000 metres and sometimes by as much as 10 degrees. This means, for example, that on top of the Munros (the Scottish mountains with tops above 3,000 feet) it can be colder than in the valley bottoms by as much as 10°C. Warm clothing may be needed, even on a sunny day, and ice may be encountered, particularly in the clearer, fresher weather following a wet spell.

Wind

It is windy aloft partly because the effect of ground friction decreases upwards and partly because air temperature usually decreases poleward. The latter causes the west-wind component to increase with height, so that gale-force winds (and even stronger winds) are more common at the tops of high mountains than at sea level. Added to that, winds can accelerate around mountains as they do around tall buildings. Over Himalayan peaks, for example, winds over 150 km/h are not uncommon in winter. Hence, climbers are forced to plan their expeditions into narrow 'windows of opportunity' - periods between winter winds and monsoon rains when the weather is likely to be good. So .. avoid the tops when strong winds at low levels are forecast, and keep away from the windiest spots, such as ridges and the gaps between summits.

On 6 March 1967, there was a gust of wind of 232 km/h at the Cairngorms Weather Station, Scotland, altitude 1,074 metres.

Cloud and precipitation

Mountain tops are often in cloud, spoiling the view and leading to a risk of getting lost. Clouds are formed by condensation in rising air, and the cloud base is lower in moist air than in dry. Air is particularly moist when the wind blows from the sea or when there is persistent rain. In the British Isles, the cloud base is usually below 1000 metres, often much below, so it is no wonder that clouds envelop our mountains, especially as they are mostly in the west and the first to be affected by rain areas sweeping in from the Atlantic. Clouds can be supercooled, i.e. their water remaining liquid even when the temperature is below freezing. The droplets in such clouds freeze when they hit fence posts, rocks and vegetation - indeed anything that stands up into wind, including people! The soft ice can build up over hours or days into a thick deposit of rime that can cause as much difficulty as lying snow.

The rain and snow that fall from nimbostratus clouds - and sometimes even passing showers from cumulonimbus clouds - tend to be heavier and longer-lasting over mountains than over nearby low-lands. This is because winds are lifted over the windward sides of mountains, causing clouds to become more dense, and raindrops larger, over windward slopes than over lee slopes. However, strong winds may blow the falling drops over to the leeward side before they can reach the ground, so the heaviest rain need not be over the highest ground.

Persistent driving rain in strong winds requires adequately waterproofed clothing. Keep a look-out for deep depressions approaching from the west, as they bring rain and strong winds. Thunderstorms are certainly impressive among mountains, but there is a risk of lightning strikes in high places. Avoid the tops if thunder is likely. Watch for tell-tale clouds, particularly those approaching from upwind.

Snow on the hills makes a pretty scene, but it makes skiing and navigation more difficult. Because temperatures decrease upwards on average, snow becomes more likely than rain at greater heights. In fact, much of our rain starts off aloft as snow, melting as it falls. So, particularly in winter, do not be surprised to find snow falling on the tops when there is only rain in the valleys. Snow combined with strong wind (a blizzard) can be life-threatening. Drifting greatly reduces progress; and the risk of wind chill makes it unwise to wait 'until the worst is over'. Avoid the hills when a blizzard is likely. In winter, the left side of a depression tracking across Britain is a likely place for a blizzard over high ground.

Three day weather forecast for Cairngorm

Cairngorm Weather Summary:
A heavy fall of snow, heaviest during Wed afternoon. Temperatures will be below freezing (max -2°C on Thu morning, min -5°C on Tue night). Winds decreasing (gales from the NNE on Tue night, light winds from the ESE by Wed night).

	Tue Morning	Tue Afternoon	Tue Night	Wed Morning	Wed Afternoon	Wed Night	Thu Morning	Thu Afternoon	Thu Night
Wind (km/h)	50	55	60	60	45	8	20	25	25
Summary	Moderate Snow	Moderate Snow	Heavy Snow	Light Snow	Moderate Snow	Light Snow	Snow Showers	Light Snow	Snow Showers
Snow (cm)	6	5	12	5	8	1	-	-	-
Rain (cm)	-	-	-	-	-	-	-	-	-
Max (°C)	-3	-3	-4	-4	-3	-3	-2	-2	-2
Min (°C)	-4	-4	-5	-4	-3	-5	-3	-2	-3
WChill (°C)	-14	-14	-16	-14	-12	-10	-9	-8	-9
Freezing level (m)	350	350	200	250	400	500	350	550	550

The following report is from the Cairngorm Mountain web site for day 1 of the above 3 day weather report.

Conditions: Tuesday. MOUNTAIN RAILWAY AND SKI AREA CLOSED DUE TO HIGH WINDS AND HEAVY SNOW. We will update and review the conditions for tomorrow wednesday by 7:15am. Weather permitting.

North Easterly winds blowing, with continued snowfall causing drifting from Sugar Bowl and above. Gusting 65mph at Top Station with a temperature of -5 C . Road Closed currently with ploughs working.

All uplift on hold with lower lifts being asessed.

2.2 Snow conditions

Depending on how cold it is, warm it is, windy it is, when it snowed the last time, how much it snowed the last time, and many variables, there can be lots of different conditions on the mountain. Here is a brief introduction to some of them:

Icy Pistes

If it is cold and has not snowed for a while, the pistes will start to get quite icy, this is because skiers and snowboarders keep going over the same layer of snow compacting it more and more until it becomes very solid. Most skiers and boarders do not like ice as they cannot dig their edges into it very well, and have very little control.

Soft Pistes

If it has snowed recently, even though the piste machines (piste bashers) will have compacted and flattened the snow, the snow will still be relatively soft. In these conditions the snow can be moved around a lot, and pistes can become very lumpy very quickly. This is when the moguls really start to be made. With the soft snow though the skis will normally have a lot of control as the edges can dig into the snow well, and it will also generally not hurt so much if you fall over.

Slushy Pistes

If it is too warm and the snow melts in the day, and then refreezes in the night, you will find that it is extremely icy in the morning, and as the day goes on the snow will start to melt, and become slushy. As the snow keeps melting and refreezing, all the snow flake structure is lost, and what is left is lots of little lumps of ice, so if you fall you will get ice burns on bare skin. Because there is no snow crystal structure in slush, slushy snow is very heavy, and can make the skis very hard to turn and move around. When the snow is wet, the water will also start to create a vacuum between the ski and the snow, sucking the ski to the snow so that it cannot slide so easily. Slush is generally not a preferred snow condition, although it can still be fun. These conditions are more common at the end of a season in the spring.

Sticky Snow

When snow is wet it can start to create a vacuum under the ski which stops the skis from sliding so easily, as can happen with slush. The worst snow for this though is generally fresh snow that still has the snow crystal structure but which is melting rapidly and starting to become wet very quickly. Because of the fine wet structure of the snow it moulds itself to the bottom of the ski very tightly making it very hard for air to get underneath. This creates a vacuum that makes it very difficult for the ski to slide. Skiing in this kind of snow can be very frustrating as skis can simply not slide across slopes that they normally would, and even skiing down steeper slopes can feel like someone has put the brakes on. Each of these conditions can obviously be more or less extreme, and it is also possible to get a mixture of the conditions. For instance if there has been a fresh snowfall on an icy piste, the fresh snow can be pushed off the ice in places, leaving icy patches amongst a softer piste.

Rime

When snow, which has a lot of water content, arrives with the wind it sticks to obstacles such as pylons, signs and fences. The rime points to where the wind has been blowing from and you can work out where there are likely to be deposits of wind slab.

Sastrugi

This too is a feature of the effect of wind on snow. In this case, snow already deposited on the ground is scoured by the wind leaving wavy lines on the snow. The vertical faces point in the direction the wind has been blowing from. In this case the wind has been blowing from the left side of the picture.

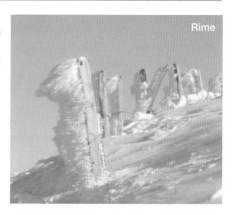
Rime

2.3 Weather Conditions

Sunny Weather

Sunny weather is generally the nicest weather to ski in as you can see where you are going easily, you can see the definition in the snow, with the bumps and changes in gradient easy to make out, and you can enjoy the views on the mountain. If it is a beautiful clear day and nice and sunny, it does not necessarily mean that it is going to be warm or even warmer though.

Sastrugi

The sunny days can be some of the coldest, especially if it is the middle of winter. Fortunately as there will not be so much moisture in the air, you should retain your heat a bit better than in some other conditions. In general though, the sunny days are the warmer days and they can be extremely warm especially in the spring. Towards the end of the season it is even possible to go skiing in a t-shirt it can be that warm, although you should be careful if you consider this as falling on bare skin can give you ice burns very easily.

Sunny Weather

Blizzard

A blizzard is the most dangerous condition on the mountain. It is when there is a strong wind and it is snowing heavily. In a blizzard you cannot see very well, the snow and moisture in the air makes you lose heat quickly, and the wind just keeps throwing more snow and cold air at you, making you cold even more quickly.

There are many different intensities that a blizzard can be, but if it is a stronger blizzard no-one in their right mind stays on the mountain, unless they really must i.e. they're stuck. Skiing in a severe blizzard is no fun for anyone.

Blizzard

White Out

A white out can be a blizzard or just a very misty day, and is basically where the weather stops you from seeing very far.and it is impossible to differentiate between the ground surface and air. In a bad white out you won't be able to see more that a few metres away from you.

This can make navigating a slope extremely difficult, especially for someone who doesn't know the slope very well. It can also be easy to go off the side of the piste without realising in places as you cannot see where the edge is if there are no markers nearby. Skiing isn't much fun if it's a really bad whiteout.

White Out

Flat Light

Flat light is where there is a thick layer of cloud in the sky, and the light bounces through the clouds so that it comes from all directions, creating no shadows on the snow.

Since the snow is all white, you cannot see any definition without shadows and different light intensities, this means that you can't see bumps, changes in gradient, or basically any shapes in the snow.

Flat Light

mountain awareness

When skiing in flat light it is advised to stay below the tree line if possible, as the trees give more definition to the snow, and act as features near the piste to use as references. Using the correct lenses in your goggles will also help a lot with seeing definition in the snow as explained on page 119. Skiing closer to the side of the piste can also help as you can use piste signs and other features as references. If you don't have much to help you determine what the piste does, it can be very hard skiing in flat light. It is hard to prepare for anything that comes up, as you don't know it's coming, sometimes you just have to hit it and hope you can recover. It can also be very hard to tell how fast you are going, you might think you are going really fast when you are barely moving, or think you are barely moving when you are actually really going some, you might not be able to tell.

Flat Light

Changeable conditions

It is very common for the weather conditions on the mountain to change during the day, or to even have several different weather conditions at the same time. This should not be underestimated as the weather can both change extremely quickly, and have two or more different extremes at the same time. In the picture here you can see how extreme sun turns into a complete white out as you go into the clouds. If the weather is likely to change at all it is very important to be prepared for it and have whatever extra equipment and clothing you would need with you.

Changeable conditions

Sunburn

Be aware that it is also very easy to get sun burnt on a mountain. The sunlight reflects off of the snow and gives you a lot more exposure to the sun than you might realise. Adding this to the fact that you are high up on a mountain and there is less atmosphere to stop the sun's rays before they get to you as well, you must be careful. Even in conditions where you can't even see the sun properly it can still be very easy to get sun burnt.

Sunburn

Temperature Inversion

A temperature inversion is a thin layer of the atmosphere where the decrease in temperature with height is much less than normal (or in extreme cases, the temperature increases with height). An inversion, also called a "stable" air layer, acts like a lid, keeping normal convective overturning of the atmosphere from penetrating through the inversion.

This can cause several weather-related effects. One is the trapping of pollutants below the inversion, allowing them to build up. If the sky is very hazy, or is sunsets are very red, there is likely an inversion somewhere in the lower atmosphere.

This happens more frequently in high pressure zones, where the gradual sinking of air in the high pressure dome typically causes an inversion to form at the base of a sinking layer of air. Another effect is making clouds spread out and take on a flattened appearance.

Still another effect is to prevent thunderstorms from forming. Even in an air mass that is hot and humid in the lowest layers, thunderstorms will be prevented if an inversion is keeping this air from rising. Sometimes you look out of the window in the morning and it looks misty. This could be a temperature inversion and when you go up the mountain it is a clear day.

2.4 Weather's effect on people

2.4.1 Wind Chill

Even when temperatures are about average, strong northeasterly winds can make it feel bitterly cold in the UK. Such a wind is often described as a 'lazy' wind, as it does not appear to go around you, but straight through you instead! In such conditions weather forecasters often mention "the wind-chill". Wind-chill is a measure of the amount of heat lost from the skin as the wind blows across it. Strictly speaking, the comparison is between an unclothed individual moving through calm air at a brisk walking pace and that same individual moving through wind.

Early wind-chill development was based on conditions likely to be encountered in Antarctica. Frostbite is a major hazard to anyone working in such areas. It was found that wind speed was critical to formation of frostbite; whilst it was possible to work in temperatures below minus 40 Celsius, winds of as little as three or four knots can make a dramatic difference. So in calm air a temperature of 0 Celsius feels like 0 Celsius. But if there is a wind of ten knots blowing it will feel the same as minus five Celsius feels in calm air. As the wind increases to 25 knots, the wind-chill falls to minus 12 Celsius. A wind of 40 knots gives a wind-chill of minus 16 Celsius. But remember, the wind-chill will not make the air temperature alter. The wind-chill factor also takes no account of humidity. When the air temperature is well below freezing the amount of moisture that can be held in the air is very low. This is one reason why skiers often find that they are quite comfortable skiing in a tee-shirt and jacket despite temperatures of minus ten Celsius or even lower, as long as there is no wind.

There is more than one way of calculating a wind-chill index. Met Office forecasters used to use the index devised by R.G. Steadman. While forecasters found it accurate for UK conditions, it measured 'full-body wind chill' and was thought to exaggerate wind chill as it excludes heat generated by metabolism, heat retention by clothing and heat loss due to respiration and conduction. The JAG/TI algorithm is now used, which measures 'face only wind chill' and is a Canadian method. The Met Office use this method as it has been clinically tested, it is simple to use and based on current research. The typical weather scenario for referring to wind-chill temperatures is a wintertime east to northeasterly wind, driven across Scandinavia or Russia, on the southern side of a high pressure system. Such winds are cold because of their track across the mountains and tundra. They can often be strong too, because low pressure over Southern Europe can result in a very tight 'squeezing' of the isobars.

Use the chart below to work out the windchill effect.

	Temperature (degrees Celsius)												
	10 °C	5 °C	0 °C	-5 °C	-10 °C	-15 °C	-20 °C	-25 °C	-30 °C	-35 °C	-40 °C	-45 °C	-50°C
10 km/h	8.6	2.7	-3.3	-9.3	-15.3	-21.1	-27.2	-33.2	-39.2	-45.1	-51.1	-57.1	-63.0
15 km/h	7.9	1.7	-4.4	-10.6	-16.7	-22.9	-29.1	-35.2	-41.4	-47.6	-53.7	-59.9	-66.1
20 km/h	7.4	1.1	-5.2	-11.6	-17.9	-24.2	-30.5	-36.8	-43.1	-49.4	-55.7	-62.0	-68.3
25 km/h	6.9	0.5	-5.9	-12.3	-18.8	-25.2	-31.6	-38.0	-44.5	-50.9	-57.3	-63.7	-70.2
30 km/h	6.6	0.1	-6.5	-13.0	-19.5	-26.0	-32.6	-39.1	-45.6	-52.1	-58.7	-65.2	-71.7
35 km/h	6.3	-0.4	-7.0	-13.6	-20.2	-26.8	-33.4	-40.0	-46.6	-53.2	-59.8	-66.4	-73.1
40 km/h	6.0	-0.7	-7.4	-14.1	-20.8	-27.4	-34.1	-40.8	-47.5	-54.2	-60.9	-67.6	-74.2
45 km/h	5.7	-1.0	-7.8	-14.5	-21.3	-28.0	-34.8	-41.5	-48.3	-55.1	-61.8	-68.6	-75.3
50 km/h	5.5	-1.3	-8.1	-15.0	-21.8	-28.6	-35.4	-42.2	-49.0	-55.8	-62.7	-69.5	-76.3
55 km/h	5.3	-1.6	-8.5	-15.3	-22.2	-29.1	-36.0	-42.8	-49.7	-56.6	-63.4	-70.3	-77.2
60 km/h	5.1	-1.8	-8.8	-15.7	-22.6	-29.5	-36.5	-43.4	-50.3	-57.2	-64.2	-71.1	-78.0

2.4.2 Hypothermia

Hypothermia occurs when a person's normal body temperature of around 37°C (98.6°F) drops below 35°C (95°F).It is usually caused by being in a cold environment. It can be triggered by a combination of things, including prolonged exposure to cold (such as staying outdoors in cold conditions or in a poorly heated room for a long time), rain, wind, sweat, inactivity or being in cold water.

Types of hypothermia
There are different types of hypothermia, which depend on how quickly the body loses heat.
- Acute or immersion hypothermia occurs when a person loses heat very rapidly, for example by falling into cold water.
- Exhaustion hypothermia occurs when a person's body is so tired it can no longer generate heat.
- Chronic hypothermia is when heat loss occurs slowly over time. This is common in elderly people living in a poorly heated house, or in people sleeping rough.

When your body gets cold, the normal response is to warm up by becoming more active, putting on more layers or moving indoors. But if exposure to the cold continues, your body's automatic defence system will try to prevent any further heat loss by:
- shivering (which keeps the major organs at normal temperature),
- restricting blood flow to the skin, and
- releasing hormones to generate heat.

After prolonged exposure to the cold, these responses are not enough to maintain body temperature, as they also drain energy. When the body's energy is exhausted, it slowly starts to shut down. Shivering stops and your heartbeat begins to slow. This life-threatening stage can develop very quickly, so it is vital that hypothermia is treated as a medical emergency.

Symptoms of hypothermia
The symptoms of hypothermia depend on how cold the environment is and how long you are exposed for. Severe hypothermia needs urgent medical treatment in hospital. Shivering is a good guide to how severe the condition is. If the person can stop shivering on their own, the hypothermia is mild, but if they cannot stop shivering, it is moderate to severe.

mountain awareness

Mild cases
In mild cases, symptoms include:
- shivering,
- feeling cold,
- low energy,
- discomfort at higher temperatures than normal, or cold, pale skin.

Moderate cases
The symptoms of moderate hypothermia include:
- violent, uncontrollable shivering,
- being unable to think or pay attention,
- confusion (some people don't realise they are affected),
- loss of judgement and reasoning,
- difficulty moving around or stumbling (weakness),
- feeling afraid,
- memory loss,
- fumbling hands and loss of coordination,
- drowsiness,
- slurred speech,
- listlessness and indifference, or
- slow, shallow breathing and a weak pulse.

Severe cases
The symptoms of severe hypothermia include:
- loss of control of hands, feet, and limbs,
- uncontrollable shivering that suddenly stops,
- unconsciousness,
- shallow or no breathing,
- weak, irregular or no pulse,
- stiff muscles, and
- dilated pupils.

Although hypothermia is defined as occuring when the body temperature drops below 35°C (95°F), mild hypothermia can start at higher body temperatures.

Treating hypothermia
Hypothermia is treated by preventing further heat being lost and by gently warming the patient. As hypothermia can be a life-threatening condition, seek medical attention as soon as possible. Follow the advice below to prevent further loss of heat.

Things to do for hypothermia:
- Move the person indoors, or somewhere warm, as soon as possible.
- Once sheltered, gently remove any wet clothing and dry the person.
- Wrap them in blankets, towels, jackets (whatever you have), protecting the head and torso first.
- Your own body heat can help someone with hypothermia. Hug them gently.
- Increase activity if possible, but not to the point where sweating occurs, as that cools the skin down again.
- If possible, give the person warm drinks (but not alcohol) or high energy foods, such as chocolate, to help warm them up.
- Once body temperature has increased, keep the person warm and dry.

It is important to handle anyone that has hypothermia very gently and carefully.

Things you should NOT do:
- Don't warm up using a bath, as this may send cold blood from the body's surfaces to the heart or brain too suddenly, causing a stroke or heart attack.
- Don't apply direct heat (hot water or a heating pad, for example) to the arms and legs, as this forces cold blood back to the major organs, making the condition worse.
- Don't give the person alcohol to drink, as this will decrease the body's ability to retain heat.
- Don't rub or massage the person's skin, as this can cause the blood vessels to widen and decrease the body's ability to retain heat. In severe cases of hypothermia there is also a risk of heart attack.

Severe hypothermia needs urgent medical treatment in hospital. Shivering is a good guide to how severe the hypothermia is. If the person can stop shivering of their own accord, hypothermia is mild, but if they cannot stop shivering, it is moderate to severe. As the body temperature decreases further, shivering will stop completely. The heart rate will slow and a person will gradually lose consciousness. When unconscious, a person will not appear to have a pulse or be breathing. Emergency assistance should be sought immediately and CPR provided while the person is warmed. CPR is an emergency procedure, consisting of mouth-to-mouth resuscitation and chest compression.

Medical treatment warms up the body from the inside. Doctors do this by giving warm fluids intravenously (through a vein)

Preventing hypothermia
Below are things you can do to avoid hypothermia:
- If the weather is cold, dress appropriately before you go outside. Even if the rest of the body is covered up, significant amounts of body heat can be lost through the head, so wear a warm hat.
- Children do not always realise how cold they are when outdoors, so wrap them up well.
- Layers of clothing trap air, which helps to keep you warm. Tightly woven, waterproof clothes are best when outside.

- Drink plenty of fluids and hot drinks (not alcohol) and eat regular, balanced meals to give you energy.
- Keep active when it is cold, but not to the point where you are sweating. If you exercise outdoors in the winter and get sweaty from this, make sure you dry off and put on warm clothes immediately after.
- Keep dry and change out of wet clothes as soon as possible. Wet clothes lose about 90% of their insulating power.
- Cut down on alcohol, caffeine and nicotine as all three aggravate heat loss.

2.4.3 Frostnip and Frostbite

Frost Nip

Most often observed at the end of the nose, tops of the ears or possibly fingers. The skin goes an unnatural looking "pasty white" colour and loses sensation. This is caused by a lack of blood flow to those regions because they are losing so much heat. Frost nip is an early warning sign that if left will lead to frostbite. This is most noticeable on exposed parts of the face such as cheeks and chin it can be readily corrected however by putting on extra clothing. An immediate treatment is to cover the affected part by a gloved hand and retreat indoors. The important thing with frost nip is to keep an eye on your companions as it is so easy to miss it on yourself. Frost nip can actually freeze the surface layers of the skin and lead to symptoms like sun burn with the warmed skin later turning bright red and being sloughed off. There is no permanent damage.

Frost Bite

Left unattended, frost nip will lead to frost bite. The difference is that in frost bite, the skin actually falls below freezing point and ice crystals form within the live cells of the skin killing them in the process. On rewarming, the skin swells and blisters turning blue-purple to black - this then forms a hardened black carapace. If the damage is not severe, the dead layer is sloughed off revealing new healthy skin that has grown underneath. It is however very painful. This is known as superficial frost bite.
More serious is when frostbite affects the deeper layers of muscle and bone. This almost always results in permanent tissue damage and may result in amputation of fingers, toes, even feet, hands and parts of the arm or leg. Many polar explorers and mountaineers have lost parts of some fingers or toes because of frostbite.

3 Snow

3.1 Snowpack
A snowpack forms from layers of snow that accumulate in geographic regions and high altitudes where the climate includes cold weather for extended periods during the year. Snowpacks are an important water resource that feed streams and rivers as they melt. Snowpacks are the drinking water source for many communities. Sudden melting can cause flooding.

Assessing the formation and stability of snowpacks is important in the study and prediction of avalanches. Scientists study differences between the snowpacks in polar and temperate regions, snowpack metamorphism and melting, and snowpacks impact on animal habitats and plant succession.

3.2 Snow Pit Procedures
A snow pit is a trench exposing a flat, vertical snow face from the snow surface to the ground. It allows you to study the characteristics of the different layers of the snowpack that have developed as the snow has changed due to compaction and weather changes. Snow pits are routinely used in mountainous areas to determine if one layer might slip on another causing an avalanche. Snow pits also help researchers measure the water content of a snow pack.

As snow accumulates and changes over time, it develops layers marked by physical differences. These layers are used to determine the history of the Snow pack. Layers are identified as differences in hardness, grain type, grain size and wetness.

The *new snow* layer consists of new sharp crystals lying loosly on top of the snow bank that are slowly being compacted by additional falling snow. From the time snowflakes are formed in the atmosphere until they eventually revert back to water they are constantly being changed or 'metamorphosed'.

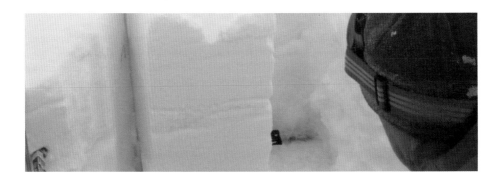

3.3 About Avalanches

Avalanches can happen wherever there is snow lying on ground of sufficient angle. Accidents in recent years in most Scottish mountain areas, as well as the English Lakes, the Cheviots, the Pennines and Wales, demonstrate the truth of this in the UK context. The vastly increased popularity of winter climbing and hill walking, along with the growth of interest in ski touring and off piste skiing, means that greater numbers are at hazard. Sadly, each year adds to the list of injuries or fatalities. Many of these accidents would have been avoidable, given greater care or knowledge, or if the victims had even paused to consider that avalanche hazard might be present.

In making practical assessments of avalanche hazard, there is no substitute for the instinctive feeling for snow conditions which can be gained only by years of experience. However, no-one is born with such experience and the novice or the less frequent winter mountain user, may still enjoy a safe day out if some basic principles are learned and acted upon. Avalanches can happen to anyone. Having accepted this, you have greatly reduced your chance of ever being involved in an avalanche. Remember that experience in itself is no antidote to avalanches and that "the avalanche does not know you are an expert!"

What is an avalanche?

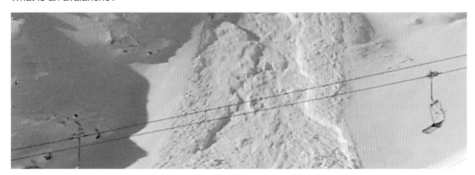

Snow is deposited in successive layers as the winter progresses. These layers may have dissimilar physical properties and an avalanche occurs when one layer slides on another (Surface Avalanche), or the whole snow cover slides on the ground (Full-Depth). An avalanche may be Dry or Wet, according to whether free water is present in the snow. It may be of Loose Snow, when the avalanche starts at a single point or a Slab Avalanche which occurs when an area of more cohesive snow separates from the surrounding snow and slides out. In practice, any snow slide big enough to carry a person down is important.

The following guidance is provided by Scottish Avalanche Information Service (SAIS):

If caught

In most avalanche situations, any defensive action is very difficult. Movement relative to the debris is often impossible. However, some of the following may be useful.

- Try to delay departure by plunging ski pole into the undersurface. This may help to keep you near the top of the slide.
- Shout. Others may see you.
- Try to run to the side, or jump up slope above the fracture.
- If hard slab, try to remain on the top of a block.
- Get rid of gear, sacks, skis etc.
- Try to roll like a log off the debris.
- Swimming motions sometimes help.
- As the avalanche slows down, you may be able to get some purchase on the debris. Make a desperate effort to get to the surface, or at least get a hand through.

If buried
- Keep one hand in front of your face and try to clear/maintain an air space.
- Try to maintain space for chest expansion by taking and holding a deep breath.
- Try to avoid panic and conserve energy. Your companions are probably searching for you.

Ski areas are thoroughly checked for avalanche danger and are made safe by the ski patrols. It is highly unlikely that anyone will be avalanched skiing on piste in a ski area. However as mountain users in a mountain environment skiers may witness an avalanche outwith the ski area. If this happens and casualties are known to have been avalanched then you have in important decision to make. Ski Patroller throwing explosive device to trigger a controlled avalanche

Avalanche rescue
If you witness an avalanche burial:
- Observe the victim's progress and if possible mark the point of entry and point at which last seen.
- Check for further avalanche danger.
- Make a QUICK SEARCH of the debris surface.
- LOOK for any signs of the victim.
- LISTEN for any sounds.
- PROBE the most likely burial spots.
- Make a SYSTEMATIC SEARCH, probing the debris with axes or poles.
- Send for help.
- KEEP SEARCHING until help arrives.
- REMEMBER, YOU ARE THE BURIED VICTIM'S ONLY REAL CHANCE OF LIVE RESCUE. Although survival chances decline rapidly with duration of burial, they do not reach zero for a long time.

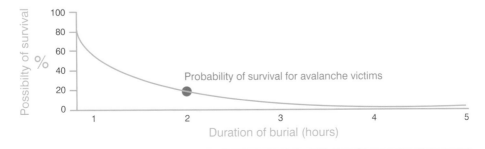

Probability of survival for avalanche victims

Possibility of survival %

Duration of burial (hours)

3.4 Avalanche Avoidance

TOP SIX FACTORS

1. Visible avalanche activity. If you see avalanche activity on a slope where you intend to go, go somewhere else.

2. New snow build-up. More than 2 cm/hr may produce unstable conditions. More than 30cm continuous build-up is regarded as very hazardous. 90% OF ALL AVALANCHES OCCUR DURING SNOWSTORMS.

3. Slab lying on ice or neve, with or without aggravating factors such as thaw.

4. Discontinuity between layers, usually caused by loose graupel pellets or airspace.

5. Sudden temperature rise. The nearer this brings the snow temperature to 0 degrees C, the higher the hazard, even if thaw does not occur.

6. Feels unsafe. The "seat of the pants" feeling of the experienced observer deserves respect. Pay heed to local warning signs

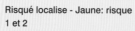	**Risqué localise - Jaune: risque 1 et 2** Localized risk - Yellow flag: risk 1 and 2
	Risque important - Daimers jaunes et noirs: risque 3 et 4 Important risk - Chequered black and yellow flag: risk 3 and 4
	Risque généralisé - Drapeau noir: risque 5 Generalized risk - Black flag: risk 5

3.5 Hazard Scale (International)

Degree of hazard	Icon	Snowpack stability	Avalanche triggering probability	Consequences transportation routes and settlements / recommendations	Consequences persons outside secured zones / recommendations
1 (low)		The snowpack is generally well bonded and stable	Triggering is generally possible only with high additional loads (2) on very few extreme slopes. Only natural sluffs and small avalanches are possible.	No hazard from avalanches.	Virtually no restrictions on off-piste & back -country skiing & travel.
2 (moderate)		The snowpack is only moderately well bonded on some steep slopes (1) otherwise it is generally well bonded.	Triggering is possible, particularly through high additional loads (2) mainly on steep slopes indicated in the bulletin. Large natural avalanches are not expected.	Virtually no hazard from natural avalanches.	Generally favourable conditions. Routes should still be selected with care, especially on steep slopes of the aspect and altitude indicated.
3 (considerable)		he snowpack is moderately to weakly bonded on many steep slopes (1).	Triggering is possible, even through low additional loads (2) mainly on steep slopes indicated in the bulletin. In certain conditions, some medium and occasionally large natural avalanches are possible.	Traffic and individual buildings in hazardous areas are at risk in certain cases. Precautions should be taken in these areas.	Off-piste and back-country skiing and travel should only be carried out by experienced persons able to evaluate avalanche hazard. Steep slopes of the aspect and altitude indicated should be avoided.
4 (high		The snowpack is weakly bonded on most steep slopes (1).	Triggering is probable even through low additional loads (2) on many steep slopes. In certain conditions, many medium and multiple large natural avalanches are expected.	Avalanches may be of large magnitude. In hazardous areas, closure of road and other transport is recommended in some circumstances.	Off-piste and back-country skiing and travel should be restricted to low-angled slopes; areas at the bottom of slopes may also be hazardous.
5 (very high)		The snowpack is generally weakly bonded and largely unstable.	Many large natural avalanches are expected, even in moderately steep terrain	Extensive safety measures (closures and evacuation) are necessary.	No off-piste or back country skiing or travel should be undertaken.

1 The avalanche prone terrain is generally explained in greater detail in Avalanche Bulletin (e.g. altitude zone, aspect, type of terrain)

2 Additional load:- high (e.g. group of skiers without spacing, snowmobile/groomer, avalanche blasting)- low (e.g. single skier, snowboarder, snowshoe hiker)

moderately steep terrain: slopes flatter than about 30 degrees steep slopes: slopes with an angle of more than about 30 degrees extreme slopes: those which are particularly unfavourable as regards slope angle (usually steeper than about 40°), terrain profile, proximity to ridge, roughness of underlying ground
natural: without human assistance
Aspect: the compass direction in which a downward slope faces
exposed: especially exposed to danger

4 Accident Procedures

4.1 What to do at the scene of an accident
This may be an accident to someone in your group or someone else on the hill.
Check to see how bad the injuries are and check to see if first aid is required.
If the injury is not serious, help the person back down the mountain.

However, if the injury is serious, place markers several metres uphill of where the injured person is lying. Cross your skis upright in the snow or your snowboard. Use other members of your group or passing skiers to assist.

Release the casualty's bindings, Make them stable and do a quick check for injuries including ABC. Send someone for help with the following information.
• Exact location (use piste name and if pylons are numbered give the number or some other information about where on the piste you are)
• Number of casualties (in the event of a collision)
• Nature of injury (do not expose skin to check for injuries) A simple statement that it is a lower leg injury will be sufficient.
• Name, sex and age of the casualty

The bottom of a ski tow will be the nearest place to go and they will be able to contact the ski patrol.

Ensure that the casualty is insulated from the snow if possible by using spare clothing and monitor and reassure the casualty throughout until the ski patrol arrives.

Whilst doing this your group needs to be off their skis at the side of the piste. Some of their skis may be used to mark off the area and some may be standing there waving arms to slow down other skiers. As soon as practical try to record the facts of the accident:

- Names and addresses of people involved and of witnesses.
- Place, time and circumstances of accident.
- Terrain, snow conditions and visibility.
- Markings and signs.

Easy Reference Guide

DO
1. Summon professional help
2. Ensure that you, the scene and the casualty are safe
3. Assess conscious level and ABC
4. Immobilise the neck (spine) if necessary
5. Keep your casualty warm
6. Gather as much info as possible
7. Constantly reassess
8. Stay calm and reassure your casualty

DO NOT
1. Rush in without checking for safety
2. Move the casualty unless their life is in danger
3. Expose your casualty to the elements unless you have to
4. Remove neck immobilisation until professional help arrives
5. Remove the casualty's helmet unless their life is in danger
6. Remove the casualty's boot(s)
7. Give the casualty alcohol
8. Panic!

Once the ski patrol has arrived they will take over but might ask for your assistance whilst moving the casualty. If the accident has been to one of your group you will have to decide what to do next. It may be distressing for some of the group members and they may need nurtured back down the piste. You might be able to continue skiing after a short break or it might be better to stop for the day depending on how the group is feeling and what time of day it is.

Consideration needs to be given to supporting the casualty, especially if you are in sole charge of the group and have no other adult helpers to accompany the casualty to the medical centre. This is one of the many judgements a leader will have to make when in charge of a group. Sometimes the injury is serious enough to warrant airlift to the hospital and you may be asked by the ski patrol to cordon of a whole piste for a helicopter to land.

5 Risk Assessment

5.1 Health and Safety at Work Act
(The source of this information is the Health and Safety Executive whose assistance with this section is greatly appreciated. http://www.hse.gov.uk/risk/assessment.htm)

The basis of British Health and Safety law is the Health and Safety at Work etc Act 1974.
The Act sets out the general duties which employers have towards employees and members of the public, and employees have to themselves and to each other. These duties are qualified in the Act by the principle of 'so far as is reasonably practicable'. In other words, an employer does not have to take measures to avoid or reduce the risk if they are technically impossible or if the time, trouble or cost of the measures would be grossly disproportionate to the risk. What the law requires here is what good management and common sense would lead employers to do anyway: that is, to look at what the risks are and take sensible measures to tackle them.

The Management of Health and Safety at Work Regulations 1999 (the Management Regulations) generally make more explicit what employers are required to do to manage health and safety under the Health and Safety at Work Act. Like the Act, they apply to every work activity. The main requirement on employers is to carry out a risk assessment. Employers with five or more employees need to record the significant findings of the risk assessment. Risk assessment should be straightforward. It should only be complicated if it deals with serious hazards.

1. Sensible risk management is about:
- Ensuring that workers and the public are properly protected
- Providing overall benefit to society by balancing benefits and risks, with a focus on reducing real risks - both those which arise more often and those with serious consequences
- Enabling innovation and learning not stifling them
- Ensuring that those who create risks manage them responsibly and understand that failure to manage real risks responsibly is likely to lead to robust action
- Enabling individuals to understand that as well as the right to protection, they also have to exercise responsibility

2. Sensible risk management is not about:
- Creating a totally risk free society
- Generating useless paperwork mountains
- Scaring people by exaggerating or publicising trivial risks
- Stopping important recreational and learning activities for individuals where the risks are properly managed
- Reducing protection of people from risks that cause real harm and suffering

5.2 Risk

Some degree of risk is associated with all activities, including skiing. Assessing and managing identified hazards which could cause harm is the process encapsulated in Risk Assessment. In simple terms, it means looking at what could go wrong, and deciding how to prevent or minimise problems that are likely to harm someone. A leader in charge of a group needs to understand how to carry out a full risk assessment and how to modify a previous one. Although a leader's principle concern is the safety of the group, a risk assessment should also seek to minimise any risks to other outdoor users whom the group may come into contact with.

5.3 The Principles of Risk Assessment

Carrying out a risk assessment is a relatively simple task once the basic principles outlined below are understood and applied to the context of skiing.

Hazard - anything that could cause harm or injury

In the context of skiing a hazard could be physical (or environmemtal), e.g. hard underfoot conditions or rocks; mechanical, e.g. faulty bindings; human, e.g. fatigue, inappropriate clothing or an existing injury or physical disability. Some hazards can be identified by checking out conditions beforehand and monitoring the condition of group members before and during a session. Other hazards can be predicted, for example through the use of weather forecasts.

Risk - the likelihood that someone will be harmed by a hazard

Once the hazards have been identified, they must be evaluated. How likely is it that the hazard will lead to an accident or harm to any group members? What is the degree of risk for each hazard? In the context of skiing, harm could occur to an individual directly through falling or skiing into an obstacle, or indirectly through being struck by another slope user. Either way, not only is an individual hurt, but the ability of the group to continue will be affected. There is no need to do calculations for this and competent leaders should be quite capable of making a sensible judgement about the relative ranking of the risks.

Risk management - taking action to reduce the degree of risk

Any risks which are considered to be high must be considered significant and require action to be taken to reduce the risk to low or to an acceptable level. For example, the risk associated with extreme cold is high; somebody could easily get hypothermia, but the risk can easily be reduced to an acceptable level by taking account of weather conditions, ensuring energy levels are maintained and wearing suitable protective clothing to avoid exposure

Review and appraise risk-controlling measures

Having carried out the risk assessment before an excursion, after the event you need to review the control measures, consider on their effectiveness and record any changes which are required. Risk assessments should also be reviewed in the light of any incidents that occur or if you become aware of new information that suggests it might no longer be suitable and sufficient. A written risk assessment needs to be dated and signed, with any reassessment date stated. Almost everyone is now familiar with the requirement to carry out a risk assessment which is no more than common sense combined with the skills of a leader. .

5.4 Types of risk assessment:

a) Generic Risk Assessment

As the name implies, a generic risk assessment concerns the general risks associated with the activity wherever and whenever it takes place. For skiing these would include condition of the piste (snow conditions), steepness of slope, safety of equipment and quality of clothing. Local authorities, outdoor centres and ski tour operators will have their own generic activity risk assessments, and the Leader should access these and confirm that he/she is happy with them.

b) Specific Risk Assessment

Specific risk assessments will differ from place to place and group to group. They require more detailed knowledge about the hazards which may be specific to the location and to the individuals in the group. Examples of location hazards include potentially challenging slopes or difficult conditions. Hazards specific to the group could be medical conditions, behavioural problems or inexperience in a mountain environment.Physical hazards can be identified by reconnaissance , which together with "local knowledge", can help to inform risk control measures.

Control measures for group specific hazards would include ensuring adequate supervision, "abiding to the skiers code of conduct" (the skiway code) and taking necessary precautions to deal with medical needs. At this stage a leader should draw up a Plan B in case Plan A becomes too hazardous, incorporating an alternative route and time schedule for the day.

c) Dynamic Risk Assessment

While the first two types of risk assessment are concerned with all hazards which can be identified or reasonably predicted, and as such are prerecorded, dynamic or ongoing risk assessment is about making judgements and decisions to cope with changing levels of risk or unpredicted hazards. Examples would be worsening weather, injuries or illness, fatigue, inability to access a piste due to closure by the ski patrol. This is where Plan B may come into use. A leader must be able to assess the situation which is facing the group and make a decision based on best judgement and the knowledge he or she has about each individual, even if it means making the unpopular decision to end the day in the interests of safety.

5.5 HOW TO CARRY OUT A RISK ASSESSMENT

The Health and Safety Executive's (HSE) Guidance on Adventure Activities Licensing Regulations (2004)(L77), states that "the scope of the risk assessment should be sufficient to identify the significant (non-trivial) risks arising from the activity". It should enable a leader to identify and prioritise the measures that need to be taken to ensure the safety of participants or others who might be affected. The scope of the planned activity must not be wider than the terms described by the risk assessment.

The law does not expect you to eliminate all risk, but you are required to protect people as far as is 'reasonably practicable'. The HSE Guide "Five steps to Risk Assessment" tells you how to achieve that with minimum fuss.

This is not the only way to do a risk assessment, there are other methods that work well, particularly for more complex risks and circumstances. However, HSE believe this method is the most straightforward for most organisations

mountain awareness

How to assess the risks

Follow the five steps

1. Identify the hazards
2. Decide who might be harmed and how
3. Evaluate the risks and decide on precaution
4. Record your findings and implement them
5. Review your assessment and update if necessary

Don't overcomplicate the process. Experienced group leaders know the risks and the necessary control measures to apply. Check that you have taken reasonable precautions to avoid injury.

mountain awareness

Sample Risk Assessment Form

RISK ASSESSMENT FORM				
Activity		Name		
Location		Date		
Reassessment Date		Signature		
Task/Activity	Potential Risk and who might be affected	Degree H/M/L	Present Control	Assessment of Effectiveness or Proposed Amendment

presentations

By the end of this section all candidates should be able to:

- Prepare a presentation on a named topic
- Deliver a presentation on a named topic
- Review a presentation and give feedback

1 INTRODUCTION

There are times when you will be required to present information about skiing. This could be briefing a group about to go onto the hill for the first time or a Parents' evening regarding a planned ski trip abroad. In order to ensure that the Alpine Ski Leader will be able to carry out such a task and to ensure that he/she has the ability to seek out information which might not be at their fingertips, the course requires everyone to prepare and make a presentation on a "named" topic. The title of the topic should be provided at least 14 days in advance of the start of the course to allow sufficient research and preparation time.

presentations

2 AIMS

i) To assist course participants to develop an ability to speak to and inform groups. This will include the researching, collation and assimilation of appropriate "topic-related" information.

ii) To assist all course participants in their completion of the Alpine Ski Leader course worksheet.

iii) To encourage discussion and debate amongst course participants.

3 PREPARATION

In preparing your presentation you should first clarify what the topic is asking you to do.
Decide on who you are presenting the information to and establish your learning outcome(s) for the session. You may use any resources which are appropriate
• Flipcharts
• Laptop & projector
• Video playback
• DVD
• Demonstration items etc.

In addition, a variety of approaches may be used:
• Lecturing
• Question and Answer
• Seminar / Discussion

presentations

4 MAKING AN IMPACT

A few quick tips to make it enjoyable for you - and your audience. And if your audience enjoys it, your presentation will be a success.

- **Know your subject.**
  If you don't, you will be hesitant, boring and unconvincing. A knowledgeable speaker is more likely to be enthusiastic about their subject. And have at least three times as much material as you are likely to use on the assumption that something will go wrong, or someone will ask the wrong question.
- **Know your audience**
  Try to find out how much or how little they know about your subject, so that your material is neither over their heads nor beneath them. Are they there out of duty or interest? Are they friendly or hostile? What are they expecting from your presentation?
- **Know your presentation aids**.
  If you are using any sort of visual aids (and you should), practice with them before hand. Fumbling with a projector or failing to find a marker pen which works will distract from your subject and suggest that you are incompetent. And don't overdo PowerPoint presentations! Keep your slides to a minimum!
- **Know your place.**
  Make sure that you have enough time before your presentation to make yourself familiar with the room and its layout.
- **Vary the nature of the content.**
  Try to incorporate most of the following to get your message across:
  - Surprise or shock
  - Humour
  - Statistics and hard facts
  - Emotion
  - Illustration and example
- **Give yourself enough time.**
  You should know how long your presentation will take, and don't go over or under the allotted time. Allow 10 per cent of the time for the introduction, 70 per cent for the main body and 20 per cent for the summary.

5 ASSESSMENT

The Course Tutor will assess the Presentation using the following Feedback Sheet. In addition, accuracy of information, clarity of presentation and argument, liveliness of delivery and interest generated amongst the other course participants will be important. Use the feedback sheet when planning your presentation and attempt to embrace as many of the questions listed as possible.

presentations

Presentation should last a minimum of ten minutes and a maximum of fifteen minutes. Presenters should be prepared to answer questions on their presentation topic after they have given their presentation.

FEEDBACK SHEET FOR PRESENTATIONS	Yes	No	Partly	Comments
Introduction				
Was the topic clearly stated?				
Content				
Was the content factually correct? Was the content logically presented? Did the presenter relate the content to the audience's experiences? Were important points emphasised? Was the level of information given appropriate?				
Personal Presentation Skills				
Was the presentation audible? Was it presented confidently? Were irritating mannerisms avoided? Was body language used to contribute positively to the presentation?				
Method				
Did the presenter involve the group? Was the involvement effective? Did the presenter answer questions effectively? Did the presenter ask relevant questions? Did the presenter gain feedback from the group? Were appropriate audio/visual aids used?				
Summary				
Was the presentation summarised? Were the main points included? Were the objectives of the presentation achieved? Did the presenter keep to time?				

presentations

Presentation Topics

Your presentation topic will be selected from the following list and allocated to you by the course organiser at least 2 weeks in advance of the start of your course. You require to attend the course well prepared to deliver your presentation

1 PREPARING FOR SKIING

1.1   What procedures need to be followed in your organisation (i.e.who you work for) when preparing to take a group away for a week to a snow ski resort?

1.2   What does a leader need to know about his/her group before departure?   Why is this information important?

1.3   How would you prepare a minibus for a weekend ski trip?

1.4   How would you brief a group of 8-10 year old children before going skiing for the first time? What should be the key points?

1.5   How can Alpine Ski Leaders comply with the Protection of Children (Scotland) Act 2003

2 MOUNTAIN AND SKI SAFETY

2.1   Why have mountain weather conditions in winter in Scotland been referred to as "the worst in the world"?

2.2   Is there a risk of hypothermia when skiing in Scotland? If so, how would the condition be recognised, treated and avoided?

2.3   Is there a risk of frostbite on Scottish mountains? If so, how would the condition be recognised, treated & avoided?

2.4   Anyone who suffers from sunburn or snowblindness while skiing in Scotland must be extremely vain and deserve all they get. Whu might you disagree with this view and how would you prepare a group in avoidance.

2.5   Mountain navigation for Ski Leaders - why can't we just follow the piste markers?

2.6   Weather forecasting for Ski Leaders - why is this an important skill?

2.7   In what ways should a Ski Leader ensure that his/her group is guided safely in the event of a sudden "white out".

presentations

3 PARTY LEADERSHIP AND EMERGENCY ACTION

3.1   You are briefing a group of young adults at the ski area.   Which points would you stress and why?

3.2   What items should a leader have available when leading a skiing group?

3.3   A member of your group has just been struck by a faster skier, out of control, and has been knocked unconscious.   What action would you take?

3.4   A week at a Youth Hostel - how would you keep your group of 15 year olds happy in the evenings?

3.5   Conserving the ski environment - how can this be ensured with groups?

4 TEACHING

4.1   "Teach a little well rather than a lot poorly" - why should you make this the foundation of your approach?

4.2   Analysing faults - the most difficult aspect of teaching skiing?

4.3   Fear inhibits safe, fun learning. How do you identify fear in your group and eliminate the cause or minimise impact?

4.4   The place of praise?

4.5   Crossing the learning plateau.

4.6   How did I do?   Evaluating your own teaching.

4.7   How would you tackle problems arising from teaching a group of variable experience?

appendicies

Activities Used to Find Ski Legs
(Day 1 Session 2)

Body Management	NOTES
traversing exercises • lean forward/back/centre, • touch toes, • head shoulder knees & boots/toes, • holding poles in front, • wheel barrow, • shuffling, • jump rebounding, • one leg, • step up & step down, • step over beach ball, • series of uphill steps	
Steering	**NOTES**
• skiddy (rotary) plough • grippy plough	
Ploughing	**NOTES**
• pressure ski • magic button, • point skis in turning direction • basketball • pat dog wave to granny • kayak sweep stroke • tractors • chinese/crabbing/drifting	

appendicies

Activities for Introductory Session
(Day 2 Session 6)

Intro to skis, etc	NOTES
• (pairs) fit one ski each then get off, • race fitting & removing ski, • same activities with 2 skis • race round circle including ski fitting.	
One ski (with or without poles)	**NOTES**
• Scootering, • follow leader + change direction + change foot, • relay race + fitting ski/change foot, • tig with one ski on. • Glide & pick up choc bar	
Two skis	**NOTES**
• moving, • shuffling, • follow leader, • turning, • getting up after fall., • side step up and down, • sliding, • various sliding tasks – catch glove, touch snow, count fingers held up, through/under gates	
Stopping (gradually)	**NOTES**
• in twos one pushing/pulling partner chips or pizza, • slide to stop in zone, • through narrow gate to stop in zone, • same but stop at pole.	
Turning	**NOTES**
• one side, • other side, • two linked, • slalom, • inclusion slalom, • forest of poles	

appendicies

Performance Profile Chart for Technical
(Day 2 Session 4 .... Day 4 Session 10 part 3)

Performance Criteria/Elements	What Is Good	What I need to do to make it better	What Is Good	What I need to do to make it better
STRAIGHT RUNNING	Day		Day	
PLOUGHING	Day		Day	
PLOUGH TURNING	Day		Day	
PLOUGH PARALLEL	Day		Day	
PARALLEL	Day		Day	
SHORT RADIUS TURNS	Day		Day	
LONG RADIUS TURNS	Day		Day	
CARVING	Day		Day	

Performance Profile Chart for Technical
(Day 4 Session 10 Part 3) What worked for me to make an improvement

appendicies

Reviewing a Leading Session
(Day 3 Session 8 and Day 5 Session 15)
What good practices would you want to use/copy from this leader

BEFORE STARTING OFF	
DURING THE LEAD	
COMMUNICATION	
ACTIVITIES	
LEADER BEHAVIOUR THROUGHOUT	
OTHER	

Reviewing a Leading Session
(Day 3 Session 8 and Day 5 Session 15)
What advice would you give to improve the leader's performance

BEFORE STARTING OFF	NAME	NAME
DURING THE LEAD		
COMMUNICATION		
ACTIVITIES		
LEADER BEHAVIOUR THROUGHOUT		
OTHER		

appendicies

KNOWLEDGE & SKILLS ←———— **self reflection** ————→ **BEHAVIOUR & QUALITIES**

Aspirant Alpine Ski Leader

appendicies

Snow and Avalanche
What to do if caught in an avalanche

appendicies

Snow and Avalanche
What to do if you witness an avalanche

The release value chart on this page has been provided by Salomon GB from the 2010-2011 Salomon Technical Manual

RELEASE SETTING ADJUSTMENT

Indicative pre-adjustment value chart (ISO 11088)

| | Chart 1 | | | | | Chart 2 Initial indicator value depending on the boot sole length (mm) | | | | | | | | Inspection parameters | |
| Skier measurements | | | | Skier Code | | | | | | | | | | | |
Weight kilo	Weight LBS	Height cm	Height FT/IN		≤230	231→250	251→270	271→290	291→310	311→330	331→350	≥351	Torsion Mz (Nm)	Forward flex My (Nm)
10-13	22-29			A	0,75	0,75	0,75						5	18
14-17	30-38			B	1	0,75	0,75	0,75					8	29
18-21	39-47			C	1,50	1,25	1,25	1					11	40
22-25	48-56			D	2	1,75	1,50	1,50	1,25				14	52
26-30	57-66			E	2,50	2,25	2	1,75	1,50	1,50			17	64
31-35	67-78			F	3	2,75	2,50	2,25	2	1,75	1,75		20	75
36-41	79-91			G		3,50	3	2,75	2,50	2,25	2		23	87
42-48	92-107	≤148	≤4'10"	H			3,50	3	3	2,75	2,50		27	102
49-57	108-125	149-157	4'11"-5'1"	I				4,50	4	3,50	3,50	3	31	120
58-66	126-147	158-166	5'2"-5'5"	J				5,50	5	4,50	4	3,50	37	141
67-78	148-174	167-178	5'6"-5'10"	K				6,50	6	5,50	5	4,50	43	165
79-94	175-209	179-194	5'11"-6'4"	L				7,50	7	6,50	6	5,50	50	194
≥95	≥210	≥195	≥6'5"	M					8,50	8	7	6,50	58	229
				N					10	9,50	8,50	8	67	271
				O					11,50	11	10	9,50	78	320
				P						12	11	10,50	91	380
													105	452
													121	520
													137	588

Note: the initial indicator values found in this table are only the starting point in the binding setting process. The initial values may need to be modified in order to achieve the correct measured release values.

NB: skiers who have had a satisfactory experience with lower adjustment values can request them.

ADJUSTMENT PROCEDURE

The release setting adjustment is obtained by using the adjustment cap or adjustment screws. The release setting is visible on the indicator. Adjust the toe piece and heel piece to the same settings. It is highly recommended to use a measuring device to check the release torque (see ISO 11088).

Release value selection and adjustment

The release settings must be used by the technician to determine the appropriate adjustment for each skier, which conforms to the following norms: ISO 11088, ASTM F 939, ASTM F 1063, and AFNOR FD S 52-448 (documentation fascicle).

SKIER CLASSIFICATION

This classification has to be determined by a dialogue between the skier and dealer, which helps to take into account the diverse factors that influence the adjustment. These factors are explained in the norms cited above.

> **Type 1 skiers:**
- Ski conservatively.
- Prefer slower speeds.
- Ski on easy to moderate slopes.
- Intermediate level, but not in good physical condition.
- Good skiers, smooth and supple style, emphasizing safety.
- Favor lower than average release/retention settings. This corresponds to an increased risk of inadvertent binding release in order to gain increased release capacity in a fall.

24

> **Type 2 skiers:**
- Intermediate skiers in good physical condition.
- Prefer a variety of speeds.
- Ski on varied terrain, including most difficult trails.
- All skiers who do not meet all the descriptions of the other skier types.

> **Type 3 skiers:**
- Ski aggressively.
- Normally ski at high speeds.
- Prefer moderate to steep terrain.
- Favor higher than average release/retention settings. This corresponds to decreased capability to release in a fall in order to decrease risk of inadvertent binding release.
- Type 3 settings should not be used by skiers of less than 22 kg.

Others skiers type

> **Type 1- skiers:**
- Skiers looking for a lower release setting than type 1.
- Recommended for beginners over 25 years old.

> **Type 3+ skiers:**
- Very strong skiers, on challenging terrain.
- Skiers looking for a higher release setting than type 3 skiers.

Skier type does not have the same meaning as skier ability. For instance, an advanced skier who skis all-terrain, but is not particularly aggressive, may be able to use Type 2 settings.

ADJUSTMENT PROCEDURE

1. **Find the skier's code in** chart 1.
Locate the skier's weight in the first column and the skier's height in the second column. If the skier's weight and height are not on the same row, select the skier's code on the highest row.

2. **This skier code is appropriate for Type 1 skiers.**
For Type 1- skiers: move up one row.
For Type 2 skiers: move down one row towards the bottom of the chart.
For Type 3 skiers: move down two rows on the chart.
For Type 3+ skiers: move down three rows on the chart.

3. For skiers who are 50 years or older, or under 10 years: move up one row on the chart.
- For skiers weight 13 Kg and under, no further correction is appropriated.
- For skiers weight 17 Kg and under, type 1- skier is inappropriate.

4. After having determined the skier code, locate the column in chart 2 that represents the skier's boot sole length (in mm).

5. The box at the intersection of the skier's boot sole length column and the skier's code row, shows the initial indicator setting for the skier. Adjust both toe pieces and heel pieces accordingly.

6. **Caution:** If the box at the intersection of the skier's boot sole length column and the skier's code row is empty, move horizontally on the same row and use the closest indicator setting.

7. **If it is obvious that the bindings release inadvertently (unnecessarily), at the request of the skier, the dealer can:**
- At first, increase the level in the forward fall, that is, on the heel piece.
- Then, only if the inadvertent releases persist, increase the level in torsion, that is, on the toe piece. Proceed very progressively in stages of half-points.

appendicies

Note Taking

Note Taking

appendicies

Note Taking

appendicies

Note Taking

appendicies

Note Taking

BIBLIOGRAPHY

The texts, DVD's and references below are additional reading/viewing matter which the Alpine Ski Leader may find useful to increase their knowledge of the topics covered in this course manual and to have as guides.

SKILLS AND TECHNIQUES
Parallel Dreams Alpine Skiing, Derek Tate (2007) Parallel Dreams Publishing, ISBN 978-0955625107

The Athletic Skier, Warren Witherall & David Evrard (1994) Atlantic Books, ISBN 978-1555661175

Ultimate Skiing: Master the Techniques of Great Skiing, Ron Le Master, Human Kinetics; Original edition (1 Oct 2009), ISBN 978-0736079594

BASI Alpine Manual Version 2.0 (2001) British Association of Snowsport Instructors

Pock'it Instructor, Sally Chapman (2004) Pock'it Books, ISBN 978-0954934804

DVDs
1) **Performance Unlimited by Mark Jones** (Endorsed by BASI)
Available from http://www.icesi.org/ & http://www.paralleldreams.co.uk/

2) **Skiing Skills - Beginners & Beyond** (SCGB & BASI Production)
Available from http://www.skiclub.co.uk/ & http://www.basi.org.uk/

3) **Skiing Skills - Piste Performance** (SCGB & BASI Production)Carving - Intermediate to Expert
Available from http://www.skiclub.co.uk/ & http://www.basi.org.uk/

4) **Improve Your Skiing 1 - Ultimate Control by Phil Smith** (Snoworks)
Available from http://www.snoworks.com/ & http://www.paralleldreams.co.uk/

5) **Improve Your Skiing 2 - Ultimate All Terrain by Phil Smith** (Snoworks)
Available from http://www.snoworks.com/ & http://www.paralleldreams.co.uk/

6) **Pock'it Instructor by Sally Chapman (Inspired to Ski)**
The Skier's Toolbox - All the Skills for all the mountain
Available from http://www.inspiredtoski.com/ & http://www.paralleldreams.co.uk/

bibliography

TEACHING AND LEARNING

Teaching Physical Education, Mosston, M., & Ashworth, S. (1994) Allyn & Bacon, ISBN 0205340938
Offers teachers/leaders a foundation for understanding the decision making structures that exist in all teaching/learning environments and for recognising the variables that increase effectiveness whilst teaching physical education.

Teaching Children to Ski, A. Flemmen & O. Grosvold (1988) Human Kinetics Europe Ltd., ISBN 978-0880111658

Captain Zembo's Ski Teaching Guide for Kids, (1983), PSIA,

Google:
- fitts and posner
- david kolb
- honey and mumford
- tannenbaum and schmidt

LEADERSHIP

Effective Leadership, John Adair (1983) Gower Publishing Ltd, ISBN 0330281003

Adventure Education, John C Miles and Simon Priest (1990) Venture Publishing Inc
ISBN 0910251398

Leadership and Administration of Outdoor Pursuits, Phyllis Ford and James Blanchard (1985)
Venture Publishing Inc, ISBN 0910251118

Leading and Managing Groups in the Outdoors, Ken Ogilvie (1993) NAOE Publications, ISBN 1898555001

SAFETY

Mountaincraft and Leadership, Eric Langmuir (1995) Scottish Sports Council - sportscotland,
ISBN 1850602956

The Weather Handbook, Alan Watts (2004) Adlard Coles Nautical, ISBN 0713669381
This book explains how to combine information given in weather forecasts with the reader's own observations to arrive at a correct assessment of what the coming weather is likely to be.

A Chance in a Million? Scottish Avalanches, (2nd Edition), Bob Barton and Blyth Wright, Scottish mountaineering Trust, ISBN 0907521592
The definitive text on Scottish avalanches

bibliography

Managing Risks in Outdoor Activities, Cathye Haddock (1993) NZ Mountain Safety Council
ISBN 0908931034

Avalanche Safety for Climbers and Skiers, Tony Daffern. (2000)
The Mountaineers Publishers, ISBN 0-89886-647-2

Snow Sense - Fredston and Fesler ISBN 0-9643994-0-7

Safety, Risk and Adventure in Outdoor Activities, Bob Barton (2007) Paul Chapman Education
Publishing, ISBN 1412920779

Five Steps to Risk Assessment, (2006), HSE, ISBN 071766189X
Download free: http://www.hse.gov.uk/pubns/indg163.pdf

**Guidance to the licensing authority on the Adventure Activities Licensing Regulations 2004. The
Activity Centres (Young Persons' Safety) Act 1995**, (2007) HSE ISBN 9780717662432

SAFETY WEBSITES
The Scottish Avalanche Information Service
http://www.sais.gov.uk/

European Danger Scale
www.slf.ch/lawineninfo/zusatzinfos/lawinenskala-europa/scale_en.pdf

Mountaineering Council of Scotland
http://www.mcofs.org.uk/avalanche-safety-advice.asp

http://www.mwis.org.uk/
Mountain Weather Information Service

NAVIGATION

Mountaincraft and Leadership, Eric Langmuir (1995) Scottish Sports Council - sportscotland,
ISBN 1850602956

Mountain Navigation Peter Cliff, (2006), Menasha Ridge Press, ISBN1871890551

TERMINOLOGY

As with most sports, skiing has some of it's own terminology, some of which may not be familiar. To try and eliminate any confusion, most commonly used skiing terms are listed here with their definitions, as well as some other physics and mechanics terms.

Piste / Slope / Trail

A marked snow path, that is patrolled and prepared for skiers and snowboarders by piste machines that compact and flatten snow, so that you do not sink into it. Pistes are graded to give a rough guide to their difficulty and steepness, here are some of the grading systems from around the world:

Europe:
- Green (France, Scandinavia, Spain) - Very easy, and gentle slope.
- Blue - Easy slope, not very steep (usually).
- Red - Intermediate slope, for more confident skiers and snowboarders.
- Black - Advanced slope, steepest slopes, for good skiers and snowboarders only.
- Ski route - Marked and patrolled off piste route.

North America:
- Green Circle - Easy slope.
- Blue Square - Intermediate slope, good pistes for the average skier.
- Black Diamond - Difficult slope, only for good skiers and snowboarders.
- Double Black Diamond - Very difficult slope, only for very good / expert skiers and snowboarders.

Japan:
- Green - Easy slope, good for beginners.
- Red - Intermediate slope, the grade of the majority of Japanese pistes.
- Black - Advanced slope, for good skiers and snowboarders.

New Zealand:
- Green - Easy slope, although they can be a lot more difficult than an american green circle run.
- Blue - Intermediate slope, for intermediate skiers and snowboarders.
- Black - Advanced slope, for good skiers and snowboarders.
- Double Black - More advanced slope, for very good skiers and snowboarders.
- Triple Black - Most advanced slope, only for very good and confident skiers and snowboarders.

The grading systems only provide a rough guide to the difficulty of slopes. In Europe blue slopes can still be far too difficult for beginners, and occasionally can be more similar to black runs from other regions, so it is always best to ask for advise on where to go if you are not very confident.

Off-Piste / Backcountry
Unprepared parts of a mountain, basically anywhere that is not a piste. If it has snowed recently the snow hear will be very soft, and you will sink into it.

Piste Basher / Groomer / Snowcat
A machine that is used to compress, prepare and flatten the snow that is on the piste.

Ski Area
A mountain or collection of mountains with lifts and pistes so people can go skiing and snowboarding.

Lift Pass
A ticket that allows you use the lifts in a ski area.

Ski Resort
A town or purpose built resort than is next to or surrounded by a ski area.

Fall Line
An imaginary line in the steepest direction of the slope. i.e. the direction a ball would go if it was dropped and fell down the slope. In many graphics on this site the direction of the fall line is shown by a darker shaded arrow in the snow

Run Out
A flatter area of snow, generally at the bottom of a piste.

Alpine Skiing
The most common type of skiing, where the both the heel and toe of a ski boot are firmly secured to a ski. The type of skiing that this site is about.

Freestyle
A style of skiing/snowboarding that is based strongly on performing tricks, jumping with spins and grabs, and riding rails.

Freeride
A style of skiing/snowboarding that is based strongly on faster and more aggressive skiing/riding, on piste and off-piste.

All-Mountain
A style of skiing/snowboarding that covers all types of skiing/riding. It is a general term that is used for skiing/riding a bit of everything without specialising in anything.

Switch / Fakie
Skiing/riding backwards. For skiing this means backwards along the skis, for snowboarding it means in the direction along the board that is not set up as forwards.

P-Tex
A polyethylene that is used to make the bases of skis and snowboard. It can come in different grades, and can also be mixed with other materials like graphite, to have different properties. It is the P-Tex that you melt wax into to make skis and snowboards slide more easily and faster.

Wax
Special wax is applied to the bottom of skis and snowboards to make them have less friction with the snow, and slide more easily.

Binding
The mechanism that attaches the ski boot to the ski

DINs/Release Values
The tension setting on bindings that will determine how easily they will release a ski boot.

Freestylers
Skiers or snowboarders that spend most of their time in a snow park (terrain park) doing jumps, tricks and rails, with equipment that is well suited for freestyle skiing/snowboarding.

Freeriders
Skiers or snowboarders that spend most of their time riding piste or powder, with equipment better suited to this kind of riding.

Ollie
A jump/hop that can be done on the flat. The skier/boarders weight is thrown to the back of the skis/board so that the skis/board bend and the nose comes into the air. The skier/boarder then throws their weight upwards and forwards springing off of the back of their skis/board and lifting themselves into the air.

Kicker
A specially built and shaped jump, for skiers and snowboarders. Normally found in snowparks (terrain parks).

Rail
A metal rail for sliding along on skis or a snowboard, normally found in a snowpark (terrain park).

Half Pipe
A U-shape run that skiers and boarders go through jumping off the sides.

Hard Pack
Snow that has been compressed down so that it will not compress much further.

Powder
Natural snow that has not been compressed, which you will sink into a lot.

Slush
Snow that is melting, after having melted and refrozen before, making it made out of ice crystals rather than snow crystals.

Ice
When it has not snowed for a while the piste will become more solid and icy, making it harder to push the skis into the snow, which generally reduces control.

Moguls / Bumps
Lumps of snow that have been created by lots of skiers turning in the same places, pushing the snow they move out the way into piles.

Snow Crystal
A crystal formed by water freezing in the atmosphere with a very fine structure, unlike that of ice.

Artificial Snow
Man-made snow, the snow crystals in artificial snow are not as fine as in natural snow, giving artificial snow properties more like ice.

Snow Cannon
A cannon that sprays water into the air at pressure to create artificial snow.

Chair Lift
A lift that takes skiers and boarders up the mountain, with them sitting on a chair and resting their skis or boards on a bar.

Magic Carpet
A moving carpet that skiers and boarders can stand on, and get taken up a slope.

Rope Lift
A lift where the skiers or boarders have to hold onto a rope which moves and pulls them up a slope.

terminology

T-Bar
A lift that pulls skiers and boarders up a slope, with a T shape bar hanging from an overhead cable.

Button Lift / Poma Lift / Platter Lift
A lift that pulls skiers and boarders up a slope, with a button shape attachment hanging from an overhead cable.

Gondola
A lift where people get into a cabin, and are taken up a mountain. There are many of these on one cable.

Cable Car
A lift where people get into a cabin to be taken up a mountain, but with only one cabin on a cable.

Avalanche
Where an unstable layer of natural snow breaks away and travels down a slope. They can be started naturally or by skiers and snowboarders, and can be of many different sizes and types

Transceiver / Peeps
A device that is used to locate people when they have be caught in an avalanche, providing they people caught are also carrying the device.

Probe
A long pole that is used to precisely location a person caught in an avalanche.

Shovel
What is carried by skiers and boarders to dig for someone caught in an avalanche.

Heli-Skiing
Skiing where a helicopter takes people to the top of the mountain. Used to go to out of the way off-piste routes.

Slalom
A race where the skiers have to make relatively small turns, to go through a course.

Giant Slalom
A race where skiers have to make turns about twice as big as in a slalom.

Super-G
A race where the skiers make bigger faster turns around a course.

Downhill
The fastest of the races where skiers take almost the fastest route down a mountain.

Gate
The flags or poles that define a race course.

Slope
An area of snow that has a gradient.

Gradient
The angle of which a surface points downwards at.

Traverse
To travel across a slope at a right angle to its gradient.

Downhill Ski
The ski that is on the downhill side as you go across a slope.

Uphill Ski
The ski that is on the uphill side as you go across a slope.

Outside ski
The ski that is on the outside of a turn.

Inside Ski
The ski on the inside of a turn.

Ski Tips
The front ends of the skis.

Edges
The metal strips down the sides of skis and snowboards, that cut into the snow giving us our control.

Uphill Edge
The edge of a ski that is on the uphill side of a slope, when a ski is pointing at least partly across a slope.

Downhill Edge
The edge of a ski that is on the downhill side of a slope, when a ski is pointing at least partly across a slope.

terminology

Inside Edges
The edges on the skis that are on the inside of a turn, or in the inside of a snowplough.

Laminate / Laminated
Where a material is made of several sheets of an original material glued together. This produces a far stronger material than the original material was.

Parallel
Where 2 or more objects are pointing in the same direction along a length.

Centre of Gravity
The point at which the overall effect of gravity can be seen as acting on, the centre of an objects mass.

Pivot
A point at which something turns around.

Friction
The force that acts along a surface resisting the surfaces movement when in contact with another surface.

Wind Resistance
The resistance against movement that is created by the air.

Dynamic
A constantly changing property, due to movement or changing inputs.